Is Inequality in America
Irreversible?

The Future of Capitalism series

Chuck Collins

———————

Is Inequality in America Irreversible?

polity

First published in 2018 by Polity Press

Polity Press
65 Bridge Street
Cambridge CB2 1UR, UK

Polity Press
101 Station Landing
Suite 300
Medford, MA 02155, USA

ISBN-13: 978-1-5095-2250-7
ISBN-13: 978-1-5095-2251-4(pb)

Library of Congress Cataloging-in-Publication Data

Names: Collins, Chuck, 1959- author.
Title: Is inequality in America irreversible? / Chuck Collins.
Description: Malden, MA : Polity Press, [2018] | Series: The future of capitalism | Includes bibliographical references and index.
Identifiers: LCCN 2017045295 (print) | LCCN 2017048494 (ebook) | ISBN 9781509522545 (Epub) | ISBN 9781509522507 (hardback) | ISBN 9781509522514 (pbk.)
Subjects: LCSH: Income distribution--United States. | Poor--United States. | Wealth--United States. | Equality--United States.
Classification: LCC HC110.I5 (ebook) | LCC HC110.I5 C5866 2018 (print) | DDC 339.2/20973--dc23
LC record available at https://lccn.loc.gov/2017045295

Typeset in 11 on 15 Sabon by
Servis Filmsetting Ltd, Stockport, Cheshire
Printed and bound by CPI Group (UK) Ltd, Croydon, CR0 4YY

For further information on Polity, visit our website:
politybooks.com

Contents

Acknowledgments

I am most grateful to my colleagues at the Institute for Policy Studies and our Program on Inequality and Inequality.org team – especially Sarah Anderson, John Cavanagh, Josh Hoxie, Bob Lord, Anny Martinez, Jessicah Pierre, Sam Pizzigati, and Basav Sen.

Throughout this book are citations from and attributions to a wide community of scholars, researchers, analysts, agitators, and organizers. My gratitude is expressed, in part, through these footnotes. A special thanks to Brooke Harrington for her work on hidden wealth. S.M. "Mike" Miller has been an important mentor over the years.

Many thanks to the team at Polity, especially George Owers. Thanks also to readers, including Colin Gordon.

This book is dedicated to all those who work each day for an equitable and just society.

Introduction

A Front Row Seat to Inequality

I grew up in an affluent family in the wealthy Detroit suburb of Bloomfield Hills, Michigan. I attended an elite boys' school, played tennis and golf at a private country club, and didn't worry for much. Though growing up in the 1 percent, my parents had a strong sense of fairness and community responsibility.

At age 26, I had a job working with tenants in mobile home parks who were struggling to buy their mobile parks as cooperatives. In the process, I personally analyzed the private financial information of hundreds of low-income individuals in order to assess the feasibility of a resident-purchase.

By the mid-1980s, real wages for the bottom half of income earners in the population were starting to stagnate or decline. Because of my job, being privy to the financial secrets of many working-class and low-income Americans, I could see at first hand the impact of declining wages. I saw how people stretched and struggled to pay their bills, from working more hours, putting more family members into the paid labor force, and taking on debt.

Because of my advantaged upbringing, I was also witness to the wealth-creating-wealth phenomenon at the top end of the ladder. I personally saw the value of wealth given to me double over a five-year period. All around me people were celebrating their appreciating real estate and financial investment assets.

In the 1990s, when I started to read about inequality trends, these were not abstract numbers on a page. I could recall the faces and stories of people at both ends of the US economic experience.

* * *

We are living in a time of extreme and extraordinary inequality. There is now a genre of research looking at different dimensions of the income and wealth gap. This body of work chronicles the shapes and facets of inequality and its adverse impact on everything we care about. I myself have written a few of these books, and have documented this growing body of analysis from my perch as coeditor of the web portal, Inequality.org.

Introduction

This slim volume will intentionally not linger on the problems caused by inequality, but instead will focus on the pathways to reversing these inequalities. This introduction will provide an overview of changes in income, assets, and the racial dimensions of economic inequality.

The primary focus of this analysis will be on the US economy and its particular systemic inequalities of income, wealth, power, and opportunity. While US inequality is part of a global trend, the condition is more acute due to the nature of hyper-individualistic capitalism and public policy in this country.

Chapter 1 summarizes the interdisciplinary research on the ways these inequalities undermine our democracy, public health, social mobility, economic stability, and civic life. In each case, I will point readers to other research on why these inequalities matter. In order to prescribe the proper remedies to reverse these inequalities, we must properly diagnose the causes. The second part of Chapter 1 examines the drivers of these inequalities and the debates as to their relevance. This discussion will go beyond the simplistic theory that they are driven by technological change and globalization, though these forces have contributed to the gap. These inequalities have their roots in "rule changes" in the economy, the result of imbalances of power and agency.

Chapter 2 will confront the significant barriers we face in reversing inequality, both in terms of the growing oligarchic power of wealth and the powerful narratives that hold inequalities in place. We will look at the current political moment in the US and the possibilities for change, setting up a more detailed conversation, in Chapter 5, of transformative campaigns.

The bulk of the book, after Chapter 2, is focused on the remedies and interventions required to shift the current US trajectory toward deeper inequalities – and reverse them. This will draw from the US historical experience of reversing the staggering inequalities of the first Gilded Age that emerged between 1880 and 1915. I will also draw lessons from social democracies that operate in the same global capitalist framework as the US but have considerably less inequality.

For ecological reasons, however, we cannot simply repeat the same playbook from the past, such as the policies that created the post-World War Two period of shared prosperity. Ecological limits to growth will constrain our ability to reduce inequality with a revival of carbon extraction and burning. As we face the realities of climate change

– and the breaching of other ecological planetary boundaries such as declining fresh water and soil fertility alongside ocean acidification – a program to reduce inequality will have to operate within the constraints of a finite planet.

The discussion of policy interventions to reverse inequality will utilize a framework suggested by sociologist S.M. Miller. He clusters policy solutions into three sometimes overlapping categories: raising the floor, leveling the playing field, and reducing concentrations of wealth and power. Chapter 3 will explore solutions that "raise the floor," reducing inequality by means of a substantial safety net and by establishing an income and wage floor that enables workers to share in productivity gains. The chapter also examines solutions that "level the playing field," ensuring equality of opportunity and eliminating distortions in rules that govern the economy and that preference one group over another. Chapter 4 will survey solutions that reduce the "concentration of wealth and power," including taxing the wealthy and instituting anti-trust provisions in order to break up corporate monopolies.

The final chapter will consider approaches to overcome the considerable barriers in terms of power politics, societal narratives, and economic theories. We will examine four examples of transformative campaigns and strategies for disrupting narratives that justify inequality and shifting power relations to reverse inequality.

Current Inequality Trends

What is the current picture in terms of our present-day wrenching inequalities of wages, assets, and opportunity?

One of the most important trends to understand, with enormous implications for recent politics, is the persistent stagnation of wages since the 1980s. After a period of relative shared prosperity, between 1947 and 1977, when real wages doubled for every stratum of US society, we entered a phase of flat or falling paychecks for a majority of US wage earners.

Since 1975, there have been extraordinary gains in productivity. But over half of US wage earners have not shared in the fruits of their labors. In 1970, the bottom half of wage earners, roughly 117 million adults, made an average of $16,000 a year in current dollars. By 2014, earnings for the bottom half of households had remained virtually unchanged, bumping up slightly to $16,200. Over the same period, the incomes of the top 1 percent tripled, from average annual wages of $400,000 to $1.3 million.[1]

The result is persistent poverty at the bottom, a work treadmill for low-wage workers, and a squeeze on middle-class workers. For more than four decades, poverty rates have remained unchanged. Over 13.5 percent of the population, an estimated 43 million people, live below the poverty line. A growing number of low-wage workers are toiling longer hours and taking on debt to survive economically.

Another form of income inequality is the increasing gap between the compensation of CEOs and top corporate executives compared to average- or lowest-paid workers in firms. In the mid-1960s, the ratio between CEO pay and average worker pay was about 20:1. In recent years, the ratio has swollen to more than 300:1.[2] Skyrocketing CEO pay is one of the drivers of increased income concentration. Between 1979 and 2005, corporate executives accounted for 58 percent of the expansion of income for the top 1 percent of households and 67 percent of income growth among the top 0.1 percent.[3]

Another alarming trend has been the updraft of both income and wealth to the very wealthiest households. Between 1980 and 2013, the richest 1 percent saw their average real income increase by 142 percent, with their share of national income doubling from 10 percent to 20 percent. But most economic gains during this period have flowed to the top 0.1 percent – the top one-tenth of 1 percent – whose real income increased by 236 percent. Their share of national income almost tripled, from 3.4 percent to 9.5 percent. Since the economic melt-down of 2008, an estimated $91 of every $100 in increased earnings have gone to the top 1 percent.[4] The bottom 99 percent of wage earners split the remaining 9 percent in gains.

Wealth has increasingly concentrated at the top. The wealthiest 1 percent of households now hold roughly 42 percent of private wealth, up from 33 percent in 1983.[5] At the very pinnacle of US wealth is the *Forbes 400*, all of whom are billionaires, with a combined net worth of $2.3 trillion. Together, this group has more wealth than the bottom 62 percent of the US population combined. The 20 wealthiest billionaires – who could all fit into a Gulfstream 650 luxury jet – have more wealth than the entire bottom half of the US population.[6]

One reason the wealthy have so much more than the bottom half of US households is that almost 20 percent of US households have zero or nega-tive net worth. This lack of any financial cushion to fall back on increases the vulnerability of mil-lions of households, including those that appear to be middle class and stable. Financial advisors recommend that families maintain three months of financial liquidity, but 44 percent of households don't have these reserves, especially if they live at the poverty level.[7]

Reflecting the historic inequalities between white, black, and Latino households, the racial wealth divide has grown over the last several decades. In 2013, the median wealth of white households was an alarming 13 times greater than the median wealth of black households — up from 8 times greater in 2010. White households had 10 times more wealth than Latino households.[8] The richest 100 billionaires have more wealth than the entire African American population: more than 14 million households with 42 million people. The wealthiest 186 billionaires have as much wealth as the entire Hispanic population: more than 55 million people.[9]

Is Inequality in American Irreversible?

The title of this book poses a serious question. Given the depth of current inequalities, is it possible to reverse the tide? And, if so, is it possible without an economic depression or a world war? We return to this question after a more detailed analysis of the obstacles, policies, and potential campaigns that could increase the odds.

The inequalities we are living through are not the result of weather events or technological changes beyond our control. They are fundamentally the result of human-created rules and policies. In the decades after World War Two, the rules of the economy focused around expanding prosperity and fostering the expansion of a US middle class. For the past few decades, the rules have been oriented toward funneling wealth to the top and the existing wealthy. We can change the rules. We've done it before in US history, as we emerged from the first Gilded Age a century ago.[10]

There is no certainty that we will succeed. Indeed, things could go badly as we drift toward greater concentrated wealth and power and the political oligarchy that results. But there are powerful undercurrents pushing us in the other direction, toward a broader societal movement, toward greater equality. The future truly is in our hands. And so this book is dedicated to our shared efforts.

1

Why Does Inequality Matter? (And Why Is It Happening?)

In the Introduction, we briefly examined the current picture of income, assets, and racial wealth disparities. Equally alarming is the trajectory of these inequalities into the future. As the French economist Thomas Piketty has warned, the US is entering a phase of "patrimonial capitalism," a society dominated by those with inherited wealth. Without intervention, we are on track to become a "hereditary aristocracy of wealth and power," where the sons and daughters of today's billionaires will dominate our future economy, politics, culture, and philanthropy.

If we view these trends through the lens of race, we see that halting progress in race relations has done little to narrow the racial wealth divide. If average black wealth grows at the same rate it has over the past 30 years, it will be 228 years before it equals the amount of wealth possessed by white households today. This is only 17 years shorter than the institution of slavery in the US, which lasted 245 years. If we stay on our current trajectory of unequal wealth growth, the racial divide between blacks and whites will double to about $1 million by 2043, the year when households of color are projected to account for half the US population.[1]

The current inequalities – and this future trajectory – have enormous implications for the health of our society. Unless we reverse these inequalities, we will become a racial and economic apartheid society, governed by a white aristocracy of wealth holders.

Why Inequality Matters

There is broad acknowledgment of this inequality data. Where there is political divergence is over the questions of "Does inequality matter?" and "Why is inequality growing?"

There is widespread recognition that poverty matters, that economic deprivation and social exclusion are social ills that should be addressed. But does it really matter, in this context, how wealthy the wealthy are? And when we talk about inequality, doesn't it lead to a politics of resentment, envy, or class war?

Some argue unequal wealth is irrelevant as long as there is social mobility and opportunity. Behind this view is the fear that some remedies to inequality, particular those with a redistributive dimension, may have unintended consequences and undermine healthy economic growth.

A growing mountain of evidence confirms that these inequalities do matter, undermining everything we care about. This warning emerges from a decade of new research in disciplines ranging from psychology to sociology, political science, economics, and more. Extreme disparities of wealth and power corrode our democratic system and public trust. They fuel a breakdown in social cohesion and civic solidarity, which in turn leads to worsened health outcomes and mental health conditions.

Inequality undercuts social mobility, the American Dream notion that you can be born in one stratum and rise (or descend) to another based on your effort. Unequal wages and assets have a perilous impact on economic stability and growth, contributing to greater volatility, including major economic fluctuations and downturns, such as the Great Depression of 1929 and the Great Recession of 2008. What follows is a primer as to why inequality matters.

Inequality Makes You Sick and Tears Communities Apart

Being poor, of course, is bad for one's health. Lack of access to medical care, healthy food, and affordable recreation contribute to greater incidence of heart disease, diabetes, and other life-threatening illnesses. But it goes beyond poverty. Public health research demonstrates that extreme inequality is bad for your health, even if you are middle class or wealthy. From a public health point of view, you are better off living in a country with a lower median income than in a country with greater income disparities.[2]

Inequality leads to unequal starts in life and lower life expectancy. Through unequal wages and wealth, societies replicate and compound health disparities, especially in the first one thousand days of life when early intervention makes important differences. As health researcher Stephen Bezruchka writes: "Tackling inequality directly would have a greater impact on health than any more direct health intervention."[3]

More equal societies such as Sweden have con-

14

siderably better health outcomes than the US. According to the US Centers for Disease Control and Prevention, the infant mortality rate in the US is 6.1 deaths for every thousand live births. Sweden has an infant mortality rate of 2.1 deaths per thousand, less than half the US. If the US had Sweden's rate of infant deaths, 47 fewer infants would die every day in the US.[4]

Americans die younger than people in other rich nations. Public health researchers at the Harvard School of Public Health attribute one death in three to high levels of income inequality in the US.[5] A 2017 study found a spike in the mortality rates of working-class whites without a college degree, linked to wage stagnation and declining opportunity. The authors of the report point to increased "deaths of despair" – from suicides, drug overdoses, and alcohol-related deaths.[6]

British epidemiologists Richard Wilkinson and Kate Pickett argue that inequality contributes to worse health outcomes because it leads to lower levels of social cohesion. Social cohesion is defined as "importance, proximity and strength of social relationships between people, groups and places across the whole of society."[7] It includes such factors as social order, solidarity, high levels of social trust, altruism, volunteerism, local belonging, and social capital.

Residential segregation contributes to this breakdown, as people are separated by race and class. US Census data reveals that, as inequality has grown, families are more likely to live in neighborhoods that are homogeneous in terms of race and class. Mixed economic neighborhoods are rare to find, while poor and affluent neighborhoods are more common.[8]

In more equitable societies, Wilkinson writes,

> The individualism and values of the market are restrained by a social morality. People are more likely to be involved in social and voluntary activities outside the home. These societies have more of what has been called "social capital," which lubricates the workings of the whole society and economy. There are fewer signs of anti-social aggressiveness and society appears more caring. In short, the social fabric is in better condition.[9]

Unequal societies have diminished social capital, which Robert Putnam describes as the "connections among individuals – social networks and norms of reciprocity and trustworthiness that arise from them."[10] The form of social capital that is most shattered in an unequal society is "bridging social capital" – the vertical social relations in a society across class and caste that are strained by differences in power, resources, and status.[11] As researcher

Why Does Inequality Matter?

Daniel Sage writes: "in more unequal societies, the differences between people from different social groups are longer and steeper and ultimately result in lower levels of 'bridging' social cohesion."[12]

As the gap between the rich and everyone else widens, it is harder for people to feel that they are in the same boat and share a common destiny. This leads to an erosion of social solidarity and the desire to make public investments that create broader health and economic opportunity for the non-wealthy.

Inequality and Social Mobility, Opportunity, Poverty, and Democracy

As inequality has grown, social mobility and equal opportunity have been declining. The US likes to maintain a national self-identity as a socially mobile society where "what you do with your life matters more than the circumstances of your birth." Indeed, in the years between 1945 and 1975, there was increasing social mobility, albeit much more for white families than for non-whites. During these years, people looked to Europe as caste societies with less social mobility.

Today, this perception has been totally turned on

its head. Social mobility is declining in the US and increasing in countries like Canada, Australia, and the Scandinavian countries of Sweden, Norway, and Denmark, according to OECD (Organization for Economic Co-operation and Development) research. The US is now among the least mobile of industrialized countries in terms of earnings. Canada, with its investments in early childhood education, debt-free college, and national health insurance, now has three times the level of social mobility as the US.[13]

One marker of the fading American Dream is the number of children who have a higher standard of living than their parents. Researcher Raj Chetty and his team found that rates of absolute mobility have fallen from approximately 90 percent for children born in 1940 to 50 percent for those born in the 1980s. If current growth were more equitably shared, as it was in the 1940s, more than 70 percent of the decline in mobility would be reversed.[14]

One implication of decades of stagnant wages is that most low-income workers are struggling with poverty wages. Half of US jobs pay less than $15 an hour and 41 million workers earn under $12 an hour, or less than $25,000 per year.[15] These workers are disproportionately black and Latino. Most of these low-wage jobs have few or no benefits, including no sick leave, vacation days, childcare, or retirement plans. These are the workers who clean hotel rooms, take care of children and the elderly, serve food, and work at retail counters and as janitors and security guards. This fuels a difficult work–life balancing act for many individuals and working families attempting to survive.

One powerful implication of inequality is that it undermines democracy and civic life. Inequality effectively disenfranchises us, diminishing our vote at the ballot box and drowning out our voice in the public square. It warps the priorities of lawmakers and blocks necessary reforms. Almost 40 years after winning the presidency, Jimmy Carter told talk show host Thom Hartmann that our political system is now "an oligarchy with unlimited political bribery being the essence of getting the nominations for president or being elected president."[16] During the first six months of the 2016 presidential election campaign, almost half the contributions to candidates came from just 158 donors.[17]

Wealthy right-wing activists have organized themselves and their money into effective associations, such as the Koch brothers network that includes dozens of donors mostly from the fossil fuel industry. They influence the political system through direct donations to candidates, undisclosed "dark money" contributions to political advocacy organizations, and tax-exempt charitable donations to think-tanks and issue advocacy organizations. Using charitable dollars, these networks have mastered "weaponizing philanthropy" in order to advance a narrow selfish agenda of tax cuts, deregulation, and promotion of sham science.[18]

Growing research points to the ways that inequality undermines economic stability and growth. Traditional economic thinking presumes there is a trade-off between equality and efficiency – and that efforts to reduce inequality will lead to a decline in economic efficiency and growth. American economist Arthur Okun argued in 1975 that societies must sacrifice equality in order to maximize efficiency and growth. Other economists argue that some inequality is required to propel growth – and that the incentives of large economic rewards spur innovation and risk-taking entrepreneurship. Policies that would reduce inequality, they argue, would be tantamount to killing the goose that lays the golden egg.[19]

A growing body of research, however, is turning this presumption on its head. It turns out that extreme inequalities of income, wealth, and opportunity are bad for healthy capitalism, economic growth, and social well-being.[20] Too much inequality is poisoning the goose.

Why Does Inequality Matter?

Several decades of stagnant wages have diminished the spending power of low- and middle-income households. These households spend a larger fraction of their income than wealthy households, so declining wages lead to weaker aggregate demand.[21] Increased consumer debt has enabled sustained consumption spending by lower-income households. But debt-fueled growth is precarious and contributes to asset bubbles, which in turn lead to economic implosions – such as the 2008 crash, for example.[22]

Macroeconomic empirical research by the International Monetary Fund (IMF) shows that inequality contributes to economic volatility, shorter periods of growth, and unproductive asset bubbles. More equitable societies, on the other hand, have longer economic expansions and stronger rates of growth, and bounce back from economic downturns more rapidly. This reflects a growing understanding by economists of the benefits of long-lasting periods of economic stability and growth, contrasted with the destructiveness of booms and busts.[23]

The IMF argues that, on average, a 10 percent decrease in inequality would increase the expected length of a period of economic growth by one half. And a 1 percentage point increase in the income share of the top 20 percent will drag down growth by 0.08 percentage points over five years, while a rise in the income share of the bottom 20 percent actually boosts growth.[24] An OECD report shows that economic growth in countries such as the UK, the US, and Italy would have been 6–9 percentage points higher since the late 1990s had income inequality not risen so rapidly.[25]

Taking a closer look at persistent racial disparities of wealth, it can be seen that they cannot be explained simply in terms of the last few decades of income and wealth inequality. The historical legacy of racism in wealth-building, however, has been "supercharged" by inequality drivers since the 1970s.

After the economic meltdown of 2008, white wealth ownership rebounded faster than black and Latino assets. This is because black and Latino wealth is more connected to homeownership, while white wealth is more diversified in financial investments. But even with this dependence on housing as a form of wealth, the racial disparity in US homeownership has been fixed in place for decades.

Thanks to public investments in subsidies that were racially discriminatory, the white homeownership rate peaked at 76 percent in 2004, while black homeownership crested at 49 percent. Since 2004, homeownership rates have steadily declined for all households, from 69 percent to 63.7 percent in the fourth quarter of 2016. For blacks, the home-ownership rate fell from 48 percent in 2005 to 42 percent in the fourth quarter of 2016. For Latinos, the decline over the same years was from 50 to 46 percent. For whites, it dropped from 76 percent to 72 percent.[26]

The bottom line is that these inequalities matter a great deal. They are the malignant force at the bottom of many of our gravest social ills.

What is Causing Inequality to Grow?

Why has inequality accelerated over the last four decades? As with a medical diagnosis, if we don't properly understand the cause, we won't be able to prescribe the proper cure. And just like with medicine, there are a lot of theories and explanations.

For example, some will dismiss income and wealth disparities as a reflection of differences in individual effort and intelligence. Economists call this the "theory of marginal productivity" – the idea that unequal compensation rewards track differentials in effort, intelligence, and initiative. In other words, I'm rich because I'm smart and I work hard. This argument is particularly popular among a newly minted class of tech multi-millionaires and billionaires who claim they "did it on their own."[27]

If this were the case, the obvious prescription would be to focus on individuals. However, this overly simple explanation excludes an understanding of the unfair starting points and advantages that some people have that others don't. Far from a small oversight, this argument misses the main driver of inequality – the economic and political system – while diverting attention onto individual behavior.

Nonetheless, people cling to narratives of merit and deservedness to explain complicated systemic inequalities of income, wealth, and opportunity. These pose a significant barrier to building popular support for reversing inequality. Later in this book, we will examine more closely the power of these narratives and how to shift them.

Among traditional economists, the most common explanation for inequality is that it is the result of skills-biased technological change. In a supply and demand economy, workers with advanced technological skills command higher compensation. Unskilled workers in the old economy are plentiful and their wages have remained stagnant or their jobs have disappeared. With this diagnosis, the cure is to invest in individualized job training, skills development, and education.

Why Does Inequality Matter?

Current levels of inequality, however, have little do to with differences in individual skills or effort. Other nations face the same forces of technological change as the US with considerably less inequality. Explanations of skill differences fail to address deeper power imbalances and structural drivers of inequality that are delinked from individual activity, deservedness, and performance.

To address the root causes of inequality – and identify appropriate interventions to reduce it – we must explore the power shifts and public policies that have tipped economic rewards in favor of asset owners at the expense of wage earners, and benefit transnational corporations at the expense of rooted domestic enterprises.

A central insight of Thomas Piketty's work – including his bestselling book, *Capital in the Twenty-First Century* – is that it underscores that capitalism, left to its own devices, creates inequalities. Through most of the modern history of capitalism, the return on capital has exceeded the rate of economic growth. Unless this central characteristic of capitalism is reformed, social and economic inequality are inevitable by-products. The period between 1930 and 1980 was an aberration in this story because of the Great Depression, World War Two, and a set of public policies, including progressive taxation, that put a brake on unbalanced wealth.

When wealth concentrates, there is a commensurate power shift, as wealth holders exercise their influence in the political system. This power shift gives rise to a set of rule changes that benefit wealth holders at the expense of wage earners. They also benefit powerful transnational corporations at the expense of domestically rooted business.

To reverse inequality, we first have to understand that inequality is not the result of optimal and efficient market forces, but of a set of rules, shaped by those with power. To shift power, there needs to be a set of countervailing political forces to ensure that rule changes promote broader sharing of production gains. For example, we've lived through several decades of "financialization" – the expansion of the segment of the economy concerned with investment and the movement of capital. At one point prior to the 2008 economic meltdown, over 40 percent of profits were in the financial sector. Some economists pointed out that this had less to do with efficiency than with the ability of this politically powerful sector to extract wealth from the real economy.

While most mainstream economists hold to a view of a pristine free market allocating resources according to market principles, a growing number of economists recognize that, as wealth concentrates, so does political and social clout, including the power to shape the rules governing the economy, such as tax, trade, and regulation policies. In *Inequality: What Can Be Done?*, the late Tony Atkinson of the London School of Economics attributed growing inequality to "changes in the balance of power." Even technological change – often considered a force of nature – is shaped by power, according to Atkinson. "Technological progress is not a neutral force but reflects social and economic decisions. Choices by firms, by individuals and by governments can influence the direction of technology and hence the distribution of income."[28] If our diagnosis is that one of the drivers of inequality is a concentration of corporate and wealth power, then, as Atkinson writes, "Measures to reduce inequality can be successful only if countervailing power is brought to bear."

In the decades after World War Two, labor unions enforced a social contract that served as this independent base of power. In 1955, almost a third of US workers were members of a trade union, ensuring that a portion of the productivity gains that flowed to capital were shared with labor. Organized labor also pressed for broader social policies, including expanded civil rights, Medicare, and anti-poverty programs that lifted up millions of non-union members. The labor movement was a key ingredient in the expansion of the US middle class in the decades after the war.

Since the 1950s, the percentage of the US workforce in a union has steadily declined, thanks in part to anti-union regulations at both state and national level. By 1977, the percentage of workers in a union was 23 percent. By 2016, fewer than 11 percent of workers were union members, with the percentage of private sector workers in a union around 7 percent.[29] As union power declined, the power of capital and transnational corporations increased. Unions were less inclined to challenge business by striking. The number of strikes declined from 371 in 1970 to 11 in 2010.[30]

Ben Bernanke, former chairman of the Federal Reserve, attributed 10–20 percent of the rise of income inequality to the decline in union membership.[31] And a study by the IMF concluded that the decline in union power between 1980 and 2010 accounted for half the increased income gains accruing to the richest 10 percent of households.[32] Previously, unions served as a counterweight to runaway executive compensation by enforcing a social contract that included a smaller ratio between average worker pay and CEO compensation.

Why Does Inequality Matter?

The power shift has also seen a decline in the power of Main Street businesses in the face of a Wall Street-dominated economy and global business. And the power of campaign contributors has increased in the face of the declining clout of voters.

The power of wealth holders has actually shifted the drivers of inequality. The growth of income inequality between 1975 and 2000 was largely the result of differentials in earning power, with CEOs and top corporate managers capturing an enormous share of compensation gains. But since 2000, the primary driver of inequality has been a surge in capital income – income from the ownership of assets and inheritances.[33] As a result of this power shift, the rules of the economy have been changed to benefit asset owners at the expense of wage earners. These rules include laws governing taxes, global trade, wage levels, and government spending priorities.

The capture of our political system by the wealthy has thwarted rule changes and led to paralysis and inaction to reverse inequality. For example, instead of passing and enforcing anti-trust legislation to protect consumers and prevent monopolies, lawmakers have stood by in the face of unprecedented corporate consolidations (see more in the section on anti-trust policy in Chapter 4). This has led to the emergence of two-tiered policies in a number of areas – one set of rules for the wealthy and well connected, and another set of rules for everyone else. Global corporations take advantage of a system of off-shore tax havens to shift earnings and reduce tax obligations, while domestically rooted businesses pay higher effective tax rates.

Reversing inequality will require both a power shift and fundamental rule changes to ensure shared prosperity.

2

What Are the Barriers to Change?

Is inequality irreversible? There are considerable political and cultural obstacles to overcome to reverse inequality. Each year that passes, the ruts of unequal opportunity grow deeper and harder to overcome. And as more wealth consolidates in fewer hands, it becomes more difficult to alter a system that benefits those who hold most of the power.

This chapter examines the considerable barriers to change, both rooted in power and political imbalances and in terms of the stories we tell ourselves about inequality.

The causes and drivers of inequality that we discussed in Chapter 1 are fixable – they are the result of power shifts and rule changes in the economy. And, as we shall discuss in Chapters 3 and 4, there are a number of interventions that could reverse inequality. We know what these are, from our own US experience of shared prosperity and from drawing on the lessons of other industrialized countries with considerably less inequality.

Unfortunately, we are at an impasse. As wealth has concentrated in fewer hands, so too has enormous political power – the power to shape the rules of the economy, block changes, and divide segments of the population through the politics of division and deflection. A segment of very wealthy individuals do not hesitate to use their power to defend their wealth through public policy and private planning mechanisms.

The political capture of our democratic system by oligarchic wealth is by no means complete. But it is formidable. Even though a majority of people want to see changes in this area, there are growing numbers of structural impediments. Partisan "gerrymandering," for example – the process of drawing voting electoral district lines – has led to greater Republican control of the US House of Representatives.

In the 2010 congressional redistricting process, Republican operatives using advanced mapping software and voter participation information – a process called "REDMAP" by insiders – redrew congressional House districts to create safer

Republican districts and a Republican "firewall" against declining GOP votes. This involved concentrating Democratic voters in a smaller number of districts, diluting their votes, and shrinking the number of truly contested districts. In 2010, there were 70 competitive congressional House districts. By 2016, there were fewer than 35. Thanks to partisan gerrymandering in Pennsylvania in the presidential election of that year, Democrats won 50 percent of the vote statewide, but Republicans won 13 of the 18 congressional House seats. Democratic voters were packed into 5 districts by design, one with an 82 percent Democratic majority.[1]

In the face of these types of barriers, it is important to remember that there is wide and growing support for building a more equitable society. Opinion research indicates that American citizens want to live in a society more akin to Sweden – with its better safety net, more efficient educational system, and less inequality than the US. And polls indicate widespread political support for policies that would move us in that direction, such as raising the minimum wage, reducing CEO pay, and taxing the wealthy.[2]

Inequality is leading to rising political volatility in the US and to the possibility of a fundamental political realignment. In this upheaval lies the possibility for a politics of transformation that goes beyond incremental reforms. Whether this translates into a politics of transformation, or a drift toward authoritarian oligarchy, is in our hands.

Tale of Two Populisms

The rise of both Bernie Sanders and Donald Trump during the 2016 presidential election can be explained by the growing inequality described above and the nature of populist movements. An unequal economy gives rise to a polarized politics.

The reality that half the population has not shared in the wage and productivity gains of the last four decades – and the anger and sense of betrayal that people feel – has given rise to both *progressive* populist and *regressive* populist tendencies. The Bernie Sanders campaign embodied progressive populism with its focus on concentrated wealth and power. The regressive populism of the Trump campaign acknowledged people's economic insecurity, but redirected its grievances toward scapegoats, such as new immigrants, people of color, and religious minorities. Regressive populist rhetoric focuses on how the rules are rigged to benefit an amorphous elite, but primarily directs its wrath toward vulnerable groups.

Regressive populism is fundamentally a deflection, sometimes encouraged by wealthy elites, to shift populist rage away from the real holders of power onto less powerful groups. This has been the historic role of antisemitism, a politics of deflection that exacerbates the differences in race and ethnicity that are hidden in more equitable times.

Supporters of both Sanders and Trump agree that the rules of the economy have been rigged, with the status quo being unacceptable for over 60 percent of the population. With a choice between Hillary Clinton, pegged as the candidate of the status quo, and Donald Trump as the candidate of disruption, voters chose change.

These populist moments have arisen throughout US and global history. The dislocations of the industrial age and the extreme inequalities of the first Gilded Age, between 1880 and 1915, gave rise to prairie fire rural populism and progressive urban reformers who advocated for the first income and estate taxes, anti-trust policies, direct election of US senators, and the passage of child labor reforms. But the same dislocations gave rise to the festering of regressive populist strains, such as the expansion of the Ku Klux Klan and nativist anti-immigrant movements. Both these populisms existed in response to the same conditions.

The seeds of the regressive populism of Trump were planted in the late 1970s and sprouted in the early 1980s with the rise of Ronald Reagan. This marked a deliberate change in the rules governing the economy to benefit wealth holders at the expense of wage earners. The corporate free trade agenda under both Republicans and Democrats – and the failure to do more than tinker with the rule changes accelerating inequality – led inequalities to metastasize. Whole rural communities and urban industrial corridors became "sacrifice zones" where livelihoods were destroyed.

The 2016 election signaled a deeper realignment around inequality issues with lessons and possibilities for a progressive populist movement. In the coming years, issue organizing and progressive candidates who effectively address these concerns will win victories and help realign our politics.

A US movement to reverse inequality should draw lessons from the 2017 turnaround of the UK Labour Party and the grassroots organization Momentum. In March 2017, Labour was facing political irrelevance, polling only 24 percent as the Conservative prime minister Theresa May, called a snap election to consolidate Tory power. But a campaign "for the many, not the few," led by Jeremy Corbyn and Momentum, completely changed the political landscape and denied the Conservatives a majority. Solid grassroots organizing and creative social media campaigns engaged millions of previously discouraged voters to fight back against inequality and austerity.[3]

Changing the Stories that Hold Inequality in Place

Building powerful movements to reverse inequality will require widespread public support and engaged constituencies. Broad segments of the public will have to understand the ways in which inequality matters to them personally and the dangers it poses for our economy, democracy, and civic life. They will need to believe that things can be better and that bold initiatives are possible.

This is challenging in the US where there is a high acceptance of inequality, as long as people feel the rules are fair and social mobility exists. But, as Canadian economist Miles Corak observed, "there is much tolerance in the US for high levels of inequality as long as that inequality arises from a fair contest in which all children, no matter how poor or rich their parents, have the same opportunities to get ahead."[4] The growing concern about inequality is rooted in the understanding that the rules are rigged and social mobility is declining.

Social movements and political leaders will have to put forward a progressive populist program of bold endeavors, like those described in Chapter 5. These movements will need to build a people-powered politics to challenge entrenched corporate and oligarchic impulses. Further barriers are the stories and economic theories that explain inequality in many people's minds. While data-based messages are motivating for some constituencies, they don't always connect with people who hold powerful stories that explain and justify inequality.

The story of deservedness can be succinctly summarized as "People Are Economically Where They Deserve To Be." In other words, wealthy people are wealthier because they got up early, worked harder and smarter all day, took risks, etc. And people are poor or middle class because they slept in, sloughed off, and made poor choices along the way.

This story of deservedness, or myth of meritocracy, has reference points in most people's lived experience. These simplistic stories, however, do not help us understand the deeply systemic nature of the inequalities of income, wealth, and opportunity that we are living through. Differences in occupation, effort, and hours may explain a modest differential in compensation. And some occupations, with years of specialized training, may justify compensation differences, such as the gap between a fast food server and a doctor. *But three hundred times more? Or a thousand times more?*

Since the early 2000s, economist Emmanuel Saez has pointed out, inequalities are more driven by differences in "return on capital" than by wage differences.[5] In other words, income earnings from wealth are a more accurate explanation of why income and wealth have flowed to the very top. This has nothing to do with marginal differences in people's labor.

The racial wealth divide, for example, cannot be explained by narratives of deservedness. Only an analysis of the multi-generational legacy of racial discrimination in asset-building explains why the homeownership rate for whites is 71 percent, while for blacks it is 41 percent. Explaining the racial wealth divide as a function of individual deservedness ignores the history of white advantage and perpetuates deep injustices.

These stories of deservedness pose a significant barrier to addressing the problems of systemic inequality. And these stories are not benign. They serve the interests of the unequal status quo.

What Are the Barriers to Change?

Disrupting Myths of Deservedness

How do we change these stories – or, as they like to say in Silicon Valley, how do we *disrupt* these powerful narratives of deservedness? One clue emerges when successful wealthy individuals don't pretend they "did it alone" and tell accurate accounts of how they got to their position.

At a press conference to defend the US estate tax, a high tech entrepreneur named Martin Rothenberg spoke in favor of the tax that he would someday pay. "My wealth is not only a product of my own hard work," he said. "It also resulted from a strong economy and lots of public investment in others and me." He described growing up in poverty, the son of first-generation immigrants, but attending great public schools, with excellent teachers, who inspired him to learn science. He walked to an exceptionally good local library, open on weekends and evenings, where a librarian took a personal interest in him. "My family had no money, so someone else paid for me to have all these opportunities."

Rothenberg recounted his debt-free college education and his free graduate school training in the field of computer science and emerging technologies. When he started a company to work on voice recognition software, he hired his employees from the computer science department of the local university. "Someone else paid for the scientific investments that built the foundations of technological knowledge I was working on – and to train my future employees in this knowledge," he said.

Rothenberg sold his company for $30 million. "So, should I pay an estate tax?" He paused and looked at the reporters. "Of course I should!" he cried passionately. "Don't I have a responsibility to pay back the society that has made *everything* possible for me? Don't I have an *obligation* – a duty – to ensure that other kids, who grow up poor like I did, should have the same opportunities for education and employment?"

Rothenberg's account is a stark contrast to the "I did it alone" stories that are often told around debates on taxation. The archetypal narrative goes something like: "I was born with little or nothing, worked hard all my years, and earned a comfortable life. I didn't get any help or government assistance along the way. I worked as the sun rose, while others were sleeping. I don't owe anything to anyone – and I shouldn't have to pay taxes."

This "Great Man Theory of Wealth Creation" is a dominant credo in our culture. Rothenberg's account of how "someone else paid" disrupts this dominant narrative, suggesting a more balanced and complete version that celebrates the role of the individual but also recognizes the commonwealth – the societal factors that contribute to individual wealth and success.

In his book *Outliers: The Story of Success*, Malcolm Gladwell untangles the many factors that contribute to wealth and societally celebrated achievement. He writes: "We cling to the idea that success is a simple function of individual merit and that the world in which we all grow up and the rules we choose to write as a society don't matter at all." *Outliers* includes a number of stories and case studies that point to hard work, but also the good fortune of timing. "To build a better world," Gladwell concludes, "we need to replace the patchwork of lucky breaks and arbitrary advantages today that determine success – the fortunate birth dates and the happy accidents of history – with a society that provides opportunities for all."[6]

A movement to reverse inequality will have to lift up these "I didn't do it alone" stories. It is not enough to talk about the policy changes required. Alternative narratives – "look what we built together" – remind us of the sometimes invisible commonwealth that makes individual wealth and success possible.

The barriers described here are not in the realm

of policy imagination. As the next two chapters will amply demonstrate, there is a wide menu of shared prosperity policies that will reduce inequality. The challenge is to shift the dominant narrative of deservedness and muster the political will for change.

3

Changing the Rules: Raising Floors, Opening Doors

There are many actions and policy interventions that will shift the inequality trajectory. And as we discussed in Chapter 2, most barriers are rooted in politics and in the stories we tell ourselves about wealth and deservedness. Without these barriers, we could advance a range of policies that would lift the socioeconomic floor and open doors of opportunity. But, as we will argue in Chapter 4, these actions will be insufficient unless we address the concentration of wealth and power.

Raising the Floor

One of the important reasons that many other industrialized countries have considerably less inequality than the US is because they have a higher floor. In other words, they have social welfare policies that establish a wage floor and a social safety net that reduces how far people can fall toward destitution. A floor is a form of social contract that ensures workers share in productivity gains and that not all rewards flow to owners of capital.

Most countries with high social floors are vibrant free market capitalist economies operating in the same global arena as the US, with disruptive technologies. For example, countries like Denmark, Sweden, and Norway have significantly less inequality than the US because they have strong social safety nets and high social floors.

During the Great Depression of the 1930s and in the decades after World War Two, the US implemented a number of policies to expand its own social safety net as well as invest in broadly shared prosperity. This resulted in the period of rising wages across the economic spectrum.

One far-reaching rule change was the creation of social security, a government-sponsored retirement program, which greatly reduced poverty amongst the elderly. Other examples include the expansion of worker rights, such as the establishment of wage and hour laws and a federal minimum wage. Laws like the Wagner Act established "right-to-organize" laws that codified protections for workers and the ability to join a union. This led to expanded unionization and the more effective enforcement of a social contract between labor and capital. It's worth noting that initial New Deal reforms did not provide protections to domestic and agricultural workers, occupations disproportionately filled by African American and Latino workers.

Investments in roads, bridges, water treatment facilities, and other forms of public infrastructure both created good jobs and increased productivity. Examples include the interstate highway system, expansion of the electrical grid, and the construction of ports and international airports. These public goods were paid for by a tax system that was considerably more progressive than what we have today. During the war years and in the following decades, the US "conscripted wealth" through a steeply graduated tax system – focused on those with the highest incomes and assets – and invested in the public projects described above that boosted incomes and consumption.

Thanks to social movements, including the civil rights movement, policymakers in the 1960s focused on reducing poverty and expanding opportunity. By 1963, possibly the most equal point in US history, there was a "war on poverty," a national resolve to eradicate poverty and the social marginalization and deprivation that accompany it.

Some of the 1960s Great Society policies were aimed at further raising the floor. These included the expansion of the social welfare state, including Medicare and Medicaid, Aid to Dependent Families with Children, and broader social security coverage for formerly excluded occupations. Investment in education increased to open up lower-cost higher education and increased expenditures on K-12 elementary school education, such as the creation of Head Start.

These government expenditures were accompanied by public support for an increase in private sector jobs through infrastructure spending. This extraordinary private sector growth contributed to low unemployment and the expansion of middle-class jobs to those previously excluded from economic opportunity. This in turn created periods of sustained and broadly shared economic growth.

In many respects, the US was on its way to becoming a society with a "Nordic" social safety net. For example, it came very close to establishing a guaranteed family income. In 1969, Republican President Richard Nixon proposed a Family Assistance Plan that would have provided a guaranteed basic income for all US families. Editorial opinion at the time was

95 percent in favor of such a program, evidence of widespread support from the 1960s "war on poverty." Legislation passed the House and languished in the Senate, and then was lost in debates around the Vietnam war and Nixon's Watergate scandal.[1]

Additional Rule Changes that Raise the Floor

Beginning in the late 1970s, the US changed direction and began to unwind some of the social investments aimed at raising the floor, reducing poverty, and establishing a basic minimal standard of material security that no one could fall below.

Meanwhile, the Nordic countries and many European social democracies continued to improve their social safety nets and commitment to policies that maintain a high floor of income, health, and basic services. As a result, these countries have greater work–life balance and quality of life for workers. OECD research shows significantly shorter working weeks and longer vacations. The average annual number of hours spent working in Norway is 1,418 and in Denmark is 1,430, compared to 1,790 hours in the US. What would you do with 8 weeks of extra free time?

In the US, one-third of workers have no paid

sick days and one-half have no paid vacation days. Everyone deserves the right to take time off when sick and to have a few weeks of paid vacation each year. In the rest of the developed world, these are considered basic human rights. Similarly, the right to join a union and engage in collective bargaining has been declining at the federal level and in many states with aggressive anti-union policies and corporate practices.

The unfinished work in the US of raising the floor includes moving the minimum wage toward a living wage. The federal minimum wage has remained frozen at $7.25 for many years, lagging behind the rise in basic living expenses such as healthcare, childcare, transportation, and housing. If the minimum wage maintained its 1968 value, it would be over $11.00 per hour today.[2] The tipped minimum wage for restaurant servers has been stuck at an incredibly low $2.13 an hour since 1991.[3]

States and localities have stepped in to fill the policy void by expanding higher state minimum wage laws and passing living wage ordinances. More than 29 states and the District of Columbia have higher minimum wages.[4] Starting in the 1990s, some local jurisdictions passed living wage ordinances that covered a targeted segment of workers, like those employed by government contractors.

Since the 2000s, more than 200 jurisdictions have passed local living wages laws.[5] While this has made a difference for workers in particular communities, it is not a substitute for a higher federal minimum wage that would cover millions more workers.

Most nations with higher social floors, including Canada and most European social democracies, have universal health insurance. As a result, they pay considerably less for healthcare, including about one-third the cost of prescription drugs. The US has moved haltingly toward this goal. The Affordable Care Act (aka Obamacare) greatly expanded coverage to include more than 20 million people who were previously uninsured. Unfortunately, more than 20 million people continue to lack coverage, primarily due to cost.[6] Obviously, efforts to repeal or restructure the ACA risk reducing coverage, such as proposals that would eliminate coverage for tens of millions of people. Moving in the opposite direction are progressive proposals to establish a "single payer" universal system. One strategy is to gradually expand "Medicare for All" coverage to more age groups.[7]

Expanding worker rights and protections is an important means toward raising the floor and sharing productivity gains more broadly. The "right to organize" has been under attack for decades, eroding the percentage of the US workforce in a union from 35 percent in 1955 to under 11 percent today. States have passed laws restricting the ability of unions to organize – and the federal government has sided with employers.

Over the last several decades, very little progress has been made to raise labor standards to protect the most vulnerable workers in our economy from wage theft and exploitation. We need to enforce existing labor standards, such as wage and hour laws, and expand protections to include paid sick leave, family medical leave, a 40-hour week, and regulation of contingent labor (such as protections for day laborers).

Two other approaches that have been deployed to raise the floor include creating a universal basic income and encouraging full employment with a guaranteed job, sometimes called public employment as a last resort. As mentioned above, the US flirted with establishing a guaranteed income in the early 1970s. A poor approximation of this has been the Earned Income Credit, which has increased the incomes of some low-wage workers. One incremental step toward a guaranteed income would be to expand this credit. But there are bolder proposals to establish a Universal Basic Income of $1,000 a month for every US citizen from the age of 18. We explore this idea in depth in Chapter 5 when we look at transformative public policy campaigns.

Countries like Norway and Sweden are sometimes mislabeled as "welfare states" with generous social welfare programs. But they should be more accurately described as "full employment states," with their focus on job training and moving all able-bodied adults toward becoming contributing and tax paying citizens. Workers who are laid off or underemployed can take advantage of extensive life-long learning programs and skills training to retool them for available jobs. The US should also explore the role as "employer of last resort." The Works Project Administration (WPA) during the 1930s Great Depression provided meaningful and dignified work for many during a period of high unemployment. There is plenty of work to be done and universal employment could be a pillar of a high social floor.

Not everyone is able to work – because of age, disability, or mental or physical illness. Part of raising the floor, in the US context, is to have an adequate social safety net of healthcare, housing, and minimal income. Raising the floor means establishing standards below which people cannot fall. The number of homeless and near homeless families in the US is evidence of an inadequate social safety net.

Without such a net, US residents live with an undercurrent of deep economic insecurity. Most of them know that they are just one catastrophic illness, job loss, or divorce away from potential homelessness, hunger, and destitution. Even the wealthy recognize the pervasive vulnerability of living in a society with a woefully inadequate safety net. A high social floor, ensuring minimum income, healthcare, and access to job training, not only reduces inequality but fosters greater security and well-being.

Level the Playing Field: Opening Doors

There is a range of policy interventions that could be described as "leveling the playing field" or "fair play." These policies and rules complement efforts to "raise the floor" described in the previous section, but are more focused on eliminating the unfair rules and advantages that give the wealthy more power and enable more wealth to flow to large asset owners. They include rules to promote equality of opportunity at all levels of society and to eliminate special privileges.

One group of "fair play" reforms could offset the unequal opportunities created by badly distributed wealth. For example, affluent families provide all sorts of boosts to their children through what sociologists call the "intergenerational transmission of advantage." This ranges from quality healthcare, nutritious food, early intervention with learning disabilities, tutors, private schools, enrichment experiences, debt-free higher education, unpaid internships, and much more.

Private family wealth now has an oversized role in sorting young people onto different life trajectory paths. And as public support for opportunity investments diminishes – such as grants for higher education – advantages tend to compound for affluent progeny and disadvantages pile up for everyone else.

In his book *Dream Hoarders*, Richard Reeves describes how "the American class reproduction machine operates with ruthless efficiency" under the veneer of meritocracy. Upper-middle-class families, not just the super-rich, aggressively shovel head start advantages toward their children, perpetuating their privileged status. He warns that, "when the income gap of one generation is converted into an opportunity gap for the next, economic inequality hardens into class stratification." The primary dream hoarding mechanisms, according to Reeves, include legacy admissions preferences, allocation of internships, and exclusionary zoning practices in residential real estate. "Each of these tilts the playing field in favor of upper middle-class children."[8]

With a growing understanding of the importance of the first one thousand days in the life of a child, there should be stronger supports for parents and accessible quality childcare. This includes parental leave policies, so parents can spend time bonding with newborns and not have to balance work–life stresses. Over time, parents need stable and quality childcare options, with subsidies for those who cannot afford the high monthly costs.

Research shows that by the Kindergarten stage, deep inequalities have already opened up between children of different economic and racial circumstances. Once these inequities open up, they rarely close. Many states and localities are looking at ways to expand pre-K school opportunities.

Another ingredient of investing in opportunity is accessible job retraining and life-long learning programs. Ten years from now, many high school and college students today may be working in jobs that have not yet been created. With rapid technological change disrupting many occupations and eliminating jobs, many workers will have to be retooled for new jobs over their lifetimes. Our current educational system, with front-end loaded schooling and occupational training, is insufficient for the new economy. Like the Nordic countries, we need life-long learning institutions that are accessible to all.

Democracy Protections, Money and Politics

Leveling the political playing field means reversing some of the partisan gerrymandering and voter suppression we have witnessed in recent years. Solutions include pressing for non-partisan redistricting commissions, litigation to eliminate extreme partisan redistricting, and election reforms. Several states, such as Iowa, have independent redistricting commissions, and voters in California and Arizona voted to establish independent redistricting processes.[9] In November 2016, a panel of federal judges struck down Wisconsin's redistricting map for being excessively partisan. The case will proceed to the Supreme Court, which may create a standard to prohibit partisan gerrymandering.[10]

The Fair Representation Act (HR 3057) would create a ranked choice voting system within congressional districts and eliminate "winner-take-all" systems. Members would be elected in multi-winner districts of up to five seats in states with more than one seat, with districts drawn by independent redistricting commissions.[11]

One force that upends our democracy is the influence of money in our political system. We need an election and campaign finance system that is buffered from the influence of wealthy donors and corporate bundlers. One approach is to support reforms that empower small donors to change the balance of power between billionaires and ordinary voters. At the national level, the current Supreme Court is tipped in favor of justices who believe there should be little or no restraint on how much corporate special interests and wealthy donors should be able to spend in order to influence our elections. The Citizens United decision in 2011 unleashed a gusher of private dark money into our democratic system. This increases the importance of reforming state and city election systems to lift up the voices of smaller campaign donors and voters.

Small donor-funded election systems are already operating in places like New York City and Maine. In these systems, small donations to candidates are matched with limited public funds. Office seekers agree to forgo donations from big donors in order to participate in this "matching public support" system. This enables non-wealthy candidates to run for office – and, if elected, be more directly accountable to their constituents, not just a handful of mega-donors.

The residents of Maine passed a citizen initiative creating a "clean election" system in 1996. This voluntary program provides full public financing for candidates running for governor, state senator, and state representative. Candidates who choose to participate may accept small private "seed money" contributions at the beginning of their campaigns. Then, in order to quality for public financing, they must collect a minimum number of $5 contributions payable to the Maine Clean Election Fund. The thresholds are 60 qualifying contributions to run for Congress, 175 to run for state senate, and 3,200 to run for governor. Once they receive public financing, they cannot accept private campaign contributions. In 2015, Maine citizens voted to strengthen the law by providing additional public funds to candidates in general elections in order to compete with privately financed candidates.[12]

The impact of the Maine system has been to make the state legislature much more accessible to non-wealthy candidates. Other jurisdictions are attempting to create similar systems. New York City has a small-donor election program for candidates running for local office – but not national elections. In Connecticut, a majority of state legislative candidates have opted in to a citizens' election program,[13] and in Montgomery County, Maryland, nine county candidates have said they'll use a similar program.[14]

In 2015, the city of Seattle passed an initiative to create a first-of-its-kind Democracy Voucher program. Each election cycle, all eligible Seattle voters receive $100 in the form of four $25 vouchers that they can contribute to candidates for local office. Prior to the voucher system, only 2 percent of Seattle residents contributed to local candidates. The vouchers enable every voter to be a campaign contributor, regardless of their income. Funds come from a property tax levy that costs an average of $11.50 per property owner. To be eligible to receive the vouchers, candidates must agree to abide by campaign rules, including a cap on the size of large donations and participation in at least three public debates. Residents anticipate that this system will create a more level playing field, including improving the fundraising imbalance between incumbents and challengers.[15]

Efforts are under way in places such as Oregon, Washington, DC, and Howard County, Maryland to pass legislation creating small donor election systems to make it possible for ordinary people to run for office and support local candidates. There are also several bills in the US Congress that would create small-donor matching systems for federal House and Senate elections. These include the Government by the People Act in the House (HR 20, introduced by Rep. John Sarbanes) and the Fair Elections Now Act in the Senate.[16]

There is a wide range of interventions, which could go a long way toward reversing inequality. But it would be a mistake to conclude that we can reduce inequality solely through rule changes that "raise the floor" and "level the playing field." While these policies are key ingredients in moving toward a more equitable society, little progress will be made unless we address the mountain of concentrated wealth blocking the way. As US Supreme Court Justice Louis Brandeis observed, "We can have concentrated wealth in the hands of a few or we can have democracy. We cannot have both."

4

Reducing the Concentration of Wealth

Reversing inequality requires policies that raise the floor and level the playing field. But we cannot ignore the rigged rules that are exacerbating the concentration of wealth.

Politically popular policies aimed at reducing inequality through "expanded opportunity" – such as investing in education – are insufficient to address the systemic drivers of inequality. The focus by some on "persistent poverty" is important, but often serves as a reframing and deflection away from the dangers of persistent imbalances of power and wealth.

Reversing inequality requires dealing with the economic and political distortions caused by concentrated wealth and power. Any policy solution, no matter how carefully crafted, will be undermined by these extraordinary imbalances in wealth and political power. And democracy will constantly be under siege in an oligarchic political system. This requires an acknowledgment that "under conditions of extreme economic stratification, there is also an oligarchic realm of power and politics that engages different power resources and merits separate theorization," according to Jeffrey Winters. "This separate realm of minority power and politics involving concentrated wealth is usually resistant to remedies based on widening participation."[1] For example, wealthy donors seem to find ways to subvert campaign finance laws aimed at reducing their influence. Concentrated wealth is like water hurdling down a hill. It cannot stop itself from influencing the political system. The only way to protect democracy and fix the system is to break up these aggregations of power.

Policies that address these accretions of wealth and power include restoration of progressive income and wealth taxes, anti-trust laws aimed at reducing concentrated corporate power, and disincentives for corporations to pay CEOs hundreds of times more than ordinary workers.

Progressive Taxation

Tax policy is probably the most important tool in reversing the concentration of wealth and political power. Tax policies serve the dual purpose of raising substantial revenue from those with the greatest capacity to pay, and also, like anti-trust policies, reducing the distorting influence of concentrated wealth. In times of war and national emergency, the US has "conscripted wealth" to match the other sacrifices that people make.[2] It's time to conscript wealth to reverse extreme inequality.

Since 1960, income and wealth taxes on the richest households have steadily declined. The US federal government, along with many states, has reduced income taxes on top earners and reformed or phased out estate taxes on inheritances. This has shifted tax obligations onto lower- and middle-income households and future generations, in the form of borrowing and additions to the national debt.

As a result, the federal tax system, while still progressive, has become considerably flatter. To understand this, we should examine the "effective rate" paid – the actual percentage of income paid in taxes – not just the statutory rate. The richest 1 percent, households with income averaging $1.7 million, pay an effective tax rate of 25 percent, while a middle-income family earning an average of $48,000 per year pays an effective rate of 16.3 percent.[3] The biggest beneficiaries of tax cuts are the super-rich. Between 1992 and 2012, the 400 highest-earning taxpayers in the US saw their effective income taxes decline from nearly 27 percent to less than 17 percent.[4] In other words, the higher up the economic ladder, the smaller the effective tax rate, reflecting aggressive avoidance at the very top.

A combination of the following federal and state level tax policies is among the most important actions we could take to reverse inequality. Restoring progressive income tax rates at the top is an important first step. In the 1950s, the top income tax rate was 91 percent, starting on incomes over $400,000 – or the equivalent of $2 million today. By 1986, top income tax rates had been reduced to as low as 28 percent. Between 1990 and the present, the top tax rate has ranged between 30 and 39 percent. Lawmakers should institute several new marginal rates on incomes above $250,000 and $1 million.

We should also move toward taxing capital gains income at ordinary income tax rates. Under the current US tax system, income from capital gains is taxed at considerably lower rates than income from wages. In 2017, the top income tax rate was 39 percent, while capital gains income was taxed at 20 percent. Super-investor Warren Buffett disclosed that he pays an effective tax rate of about 14 percent, while his secretary pays an effective rate of over 27 percent. This is because most of Buffett's income comes from capital gains and his secretary's income comes from wages.[5]

Hedge fund managers utilize a "carried interest" loophole to reclassify their wage income as capital income, significantly reducing their taxes. A simple reform would be to tax all income the same, through a graduated rate system, regardless of its source. Under these rules, low-income seniors would pay at the lowest rate of 15 percent on their retirement capital income while wealthy hedge fund investors would pay at the 39 percent top tax rate on their capital income.

We should not only maintain the estate tax, but expand its impact. The estate tax was established in 1916 in response to the staggering inequalities of America's first Gilded Age. For over a century, the US has maintained an estate tax on inherited assets with the intention of putting limits on this top-heavy wealth. As secondary benefits, the estate tax provides a powerful incentive for charitable giving and raises substantial revenue exclusively from citizens with the greatest capacity to pay. The US estate tax is paid exclusively by multi-millionaires and billionaires upon the transfer of wealth at death. In 2017, for example, a couple with over $10.98 million in wealth (or a single individual with more than $5.49 million) is subject to the tax.[6] The estate tax has a flat rate of 40 percent, but the effective rate, after deductions and loopholes, is only 17 percent for all taxable estates and under 19 percent for estates above $20 million.[7]

The estate and gift tax system should be strengthened and loopholes closed. Progressive estate tax reforms have been introduced over the years that focus on instituting a graduated rate structure, with higher tax rates on estates worth over $50 million, $100 million, and $1 billion, respectively.

States could also protect and expand state-level estate taxation. Since the 1920s, states have received a portion of the federal estate tax to ensure a more simple and uniform system. In 2001, anti-tax forces attempted to eliminate the estate tax and passed a law phasing out the share of tax proceeds going to states. Following this, 18 states took action to retain state-level estate taxes, but 32 states no longer raise revenue through this system. These include states like California that previously raised over $1 billion a year from the estate tax. Restoring estate taxes in all states could raise an additional $3–6 billion per year, funds that would pay for public investments and middle-class tax reductions.

States could also explore other forms of wealth

taxation. While estate taxes only apply to large estates at death, a state wealth tax could be levied on an annual basis. Several European countries, such as France and the Netherlands, have annual net worth taxes. While the US Constitution may prohibit the direct taxation of wealth at the national level, states are not prohibited from instituting wealth taxes.[8] States could raise substantial revenue with a modest wealth tax on households with $10 million or more. The tax would be on net worth – assets (cash, investments, real estate) minus any debts, and exempting all but the most wealthy. The rate structure could be either flat – say one-half of 1 percent (0.5), or graduated, starting at 0.15 percent for wealth between $10 million and $20 million, and rising to 1 percent on wealth over $500 million.[9]

Lawmakers should remove the cap on Social Security withholding taxes. All US wage earners have a portion of their income withheld from their paychecks as part of their contributions to Social Security. But the annual amount withheld was capped at $127,200 in 2017. This means that the highest income earners have finished paying Social Security by early January, while a person earning $70,000 a year pays this tax all year long. The 202 people who earned more than $50 million in wages in 2016 had already paid their Social Security contribution by 5:00 a.m. on New Year's Day.[10] Raising or eliminating the cap on payroll taxes would increase reserves and strengthen the Social Security system for all retirees, with minimal impact on the economy.[11]

Policymakers should explore instituting a financial transaction tax (FTT), sometimes called a "Wall Street speculation" or "Robin Hood" tax, which is a modest levy on financial transactions. While the rate is low, an FTT could raise substantial revenue because the broad base of financial transactions is substantial. The tax has the added benefit of curbing high frequency trading, which adds little value to the real economy. One proposal, the Wall Street Trading and Speculator's Tax Act, would levy a tax of 0.03 percent on stock, bond, and derivative trades, and could raise $350 billion over 10 years, according to an estimate by the Joint Committee on Taxation.[12] One FTT initiative, the Inclusive Prosperity Act of 2017, would, if implemented, impose a tax of 0.5 percent on stocks, 0.1 percent for bonds, and 0.005 percent for derivatives. Such a tax would raise $600 billion over 10 years.[13] Some financial transaction taxes could be designed to raise as much as $300 billion per year.[14] Financial transaction taxes have been implemented in 11 European countries, and support for the concept it growing in the US.[15]

Reforming CEO Pay and Corporate Incentive Systems

One driver of inequality is the explosion of CEO pay and the growing ratio between highest paid and average workers, which is now at over 300:1. Compensation committees set salaries, bonuses, and other forms of compensation based on immediate term criteria, rather than a longer shareholder value perspective. This fosters a short-term mentality and incentive system among corporate leaders and encourages actions that boost immediate shareholder prices, such as job cuts, accounting fraud, and reduced investment in research and development, actions that sometimes endanger the long-term health of a company.

Corporate governance and management experts, such as the late management guru Peter Drucker, warn that excessive pay disparities are bad for company performance and undermine morale within firms.[16] Top-heavy compensation systems foster unnecessary hierarchy, which can inhibit communication and innovation. Many information age companies find that horizontal organizational structures reward the creative contributions of all employees and spur innovation.[17]

Runaway CEO pay poses other dangers for the wider society as well. For example, CEO pay practices drove the reckless "bonus culture" that fueled the 2008 economic meltdown. And within oil, gas, and coal energy companies, bloated CEO pay promotes a "take the money and run" obsession with short-term profits – rather than a longer view toward future profits from transitioning to the renewable energy economy.

Other policy actions can change these internal corporate practices and their negative impact on the larger economy. Reforms include capping the tax deductibility of excessive pay. In an effort to reduce the gap between lowest-paid workers and CEOs, some federal and state lawmakers have proposed capping the tax deductibility of excessive pay. Currently, corporations are allowed to deduct unlimited amounts of so-called performance pay, including stock options and certain types of bonuses. This means that the more the corporations pay their CEO, the less they pay in taxes. Senators Jack Reed and Richard Blumenthal, along with Rep. Lloyd Doggett – all Democrats – are leading efforts to eliminate this perverse loophole.

Reducing the Concentration of Wealth

Lawmakers recently reintroduced a 2017 version of the Stop Subsidizing Multimillion Dollar Corporate Bonuses Act that would treat bonuses as salary and cap their deductibility at $1 million.[18] Several federal lawmakers have championed the CEO Accountability and Responsibility Act to link federal tax rates to their pay ratio level. The Act increases tax rates on companies with a CEO: worker pay gap greater than 100:1 and reduces taxes on companies with a pay gap below 50:1.[19]

What can a local community do about the dizzying inequality of pay between workers and CEOs of corporations? Some jurisdictions, like Portland Oregon, are not waiting for federal action or corporate governance reforms to close the wage gap. In 2016, Portland passed an ordinance to levy a business tax surcharge on companies with CEO:worker pay gaps of over 100:1. The Portland law amends their local business license tax on public corporations, adding a 10 percent surtax on the company's existing business license if the pay ratio rises above 100:1.[20]

The movement to penalize excessive pay gaps between CEOs and average workers is growing. Bills similar to the Portland ordinance have been introduced in Illinois, Massachusetts, Rhode Island, Minnesota, and Connecticut.[21] On the other hand, the conservative Business Roundtable has identified federal pay ratio disclosure as one of its top 16 priorities for regulations to be abolished.[22]

Anti-Trust Policy to Reduce Corporate Concentration

When a paying customer was forcibly removed from a United Airlines flight in March 2017, there was a great uproar over the ways that US airlines mistreat the flying public. Underlying the fiasco was a lesson about an imbalance in corporate power. Such an incident would not have happened in Europe, where there is greater competition in the airline industry and regulatory oversight of company practices, including stricter rules for bumping passengers.

European regulators have worked hard to protect competition, recently blocking a merger between Ryanair and Aer Lingus. In the US, however, four US carriers dominate 80 percent of the market. The 2013 merger of US Airways and American Airlines increased the latter's market share of the Philadelphia travel market to 77 percent. At 40 of the 100 biggest US airports, only one carrier accounts for half of the capacity. Europe also encourages competition among multiple airports in a region. As a result, US air travelers pay more per seat mile than European competitors, share little in savings from the decline in fuel costs, and have worse service. Of the 30 best airline carriers rated by aviation website Skytrax, only one is a US carrier.[23]

The years 2015 and 2016 were huge for corporate mergers and acquisitions, especially in beer, pharmaceuticals, chemicals, agricultural seeds, energy, and semi-conductors. According to Thompson-Reuters, 2015 was a "bonanza year," with $4.7 trillion in deals announced, a 42 percent increase over 2014 and surpassing the previous record of $4.4 trillion in 2007. These include 137 mega-deals that exceed $5 billion, accounting for 52 percent of merger activity.[24] Such levels of concentrated corporate wealth power pose a parallel set of dangers to democratic institutions, as an extension of concentrated private wealth. Corporate consolidation chokes out competition from local Main Street businesses and raises prices for consumers.[25]

A century ago, during the first Gilded Age, the early anti-trust movement challenged the great "trusts" or "combinations" that controlled vast sectors of the economy and engaged in price fixing and other anti-competitive practices. The Chicago-based meat trusts controlled all beef markets, while railroad barons controlled the lifeblood of US transport. John D. Rockefeller gained a monopoly in the oil production, refinement, and distribution markets through Standard Oil, squeezing out or buying up all competitors.

The Sherman Anti-Trust Act of 1890 and the Clayton Anti-Trust Act of 1914 were aimed at breaking up corporate monopolies and preventing mergers and acquisitions that substantially reduced market competition. This legislation was rooted in constitutional authority to regulate interstate commerce. As Barry Lynn said: "The purpose of our antimonopoly laws was to protect our communities against distant capitalists taking control of local commerce that we believe we should be in control of. These political ... goals were at the heart of antimonopoly thinking in the United States at the community level, at the state level, and later at the federal level for 200 years."[26]

In 1982, anti-trust actions against the telephone giant AT&T resulted in the break-up of the phone company into smaller companies. But since the late 1970s, government anti-trust actions have been rare and largely ineffectual. Actions taken in 2001 against Microsoft allowed the company to remain in consolidated form.

Policymakers and executive branches adopted a

libertarian conservative perspective, espoused by the Chicago School and economist Milton Friedman, that anti-trust enforcement leads to economic inefficiencies and waste. As the power of transnational corporations increased in our political system, meaningful anti-trust actions declined.

Corporate concentration hurts our Main Streets and rural communities, costing jobs and local businesses. The growth of Amazon.com has led to the shuttering of thousands of bricks-and-mortar bookstores and is now undercutting other retail outlets.

Farmers are facing a chilling concentration of agricultural seed and chemical companies. Six global conglomerates are now angling to further consolidate with the proposed mergers of Dow Chemical and Dupont, Bayer and Monsanto, and Syngenta and ChemChina. The market share for the top four sellers of corn seed increased from 60 percent in 2000 to 85 percent in 2015. During the same period, the "big four" increased their share of soybean seed sales from 51 percent to 76 percent. The top four sellers of cottonseed now control 91 percent of the market.[27] Such monopolies hurt farmers and small businesses, undermine productivity, reduce job growth, and thwart business start-ups.

As inequality has grown over the last 40 years, so

has the concentration of corporate power in many sectors that touch our individual pocketbooks. Consider the concentration of service providers and expenses that many of us pay on a regular basis: cell phone providers, bank fees, internet and broadband coverage, prescription drugs, on-line streaming, and the cost of beer.

Regulating and enforcing anti-trust will reduce inequality and enable local and regional economies to flourish.[28] Actions include reviving anti-trust enforcement. The public must demand more rigorous anti-trust enforcement to protect consumers and prevent monopolies. Israel challenged the concentration of the mobile telecommunications industry in 2011, with broad support across the political spectrum. After passage of anti-consolidation legislation, increased competition led to a 90 percent price drop in the Israeli mobile phone market.[29]

Anti-trust enforcers should stop further consolidation of the banking sector and break up existing mega-banks. In the aftermath of the Great Recession of 2008, the five largest Wall Street banks further consolidated their hold on the market and grew by 30 percent. The 15,000 community-based banks and credit unions must be protected from "too big to fail" banks.

Reducing the Concentration of Wealth

The Hidden Wealth Problem

Efforts to reverse the concentration of wealth run headlong into the growing practices of hiding wealth from taxation and accountability. As inequality has grown, so has a "wealth defense industry" that assists global corporations and wealthy individuals to dodge taxes and accountability. These wealth defenders include lawyers, accountants, and wealth managers who facilitate the shifting of assets off-shore or into complicated trusts that purposefully conceal the identity of the owners and beneficiaries.

Local jurisdictions and nation-states that want to levy taxes and invest in solutions to reduce inequality will not be able to ignore these practices. Trillions of dollars have been moved, creating unnecessary budget austerities worldwide at both nation and state level.

Off-shore accounts and complex trusts have reduced effective tax rates (the percentage of incomes that households actually pay in contrast to the statutory rate on the books). The primary beneficiaries are those who can pay for the services of professional wealth defenders.

The use of off-shore tax havens – or secrecy jurisdictions – has become more widespread in the last few decades, both for transnational corporations and wealthy individuals. The 2016 publication of the Panama Papers drew widespread attention to the use of tax havens and shell corporations among the world's wealth elites. A leak from a Panamanian law firm, Mossack Fonseca, disclosed transactions from more than 200,000 off-shore shell corporations covering 40 years of activities. Among those exposed were the president of Ukraine, the prime ministers of Iceland and Pakistan, members of China's politburo, three members of the UK House of Lords, Argentine soccer star Lionel Messi, movie star Jackie Chan, and 29 billionaires from the *Forbes* global wealth list.[30]

The US itself operates as a secrecy jurisdiction, serving as an off-shore tax haven for international wealth seeking a safe harbor. US subsidiaries and real estate investments are preferred safe havens for Russian mobsters and Chinese billionaires who need to move wealth out of their home countries, for fear of taxation or expropriation. States such as Wyoming and Delaware maintain low corporate disclosure and reporting requirements, making them ideal for banking illegal funds and hidden wealth. It's harder to get a fishing license or library card in these states – where you have to prove your real identity – than it is to create a shell corporation.[31]

Secrecy jurisdictions around the world not only

facilitate tax avoidance, but enable criminal activities such as money laundering from the drug trade and trafficking of human slaves. Drug cartels, smugglers, and terrorist networks like ISIS flourish thanks to this secret system, where the ownership identity of corporations and bank account holders is hidden.[32]

Economist Gabriel Zucman believes that the use of tax havens increased by 25 percent between 2009 and 2015. He estimates that about 8 percent of the world's individual financial wealth – almost $8 trillion – is hidden in these off-shore centers. Wealthy US citizens have an estimated $1.2 trillion stashed off-shore, resulting in $200 billion a year of lost tax revenue.[33] This estimate is probably low. Jim Henry, a former economist at McKinsey, calls the off-shore financial world the "economic equivalent of an astrophysical black hole," holding an estimated $21 trillion of the world's financial wealth, more than the gross domestic product of the US.[34]

In reality, we don't actually know the exact amount of individual wealth that has been shifted off-shore because of the use of trusts to obscure ownership (more about these in a moment). With public corporations, there is more information about their tax avoidance exploits because of public filings in the US and other countries. As a result, we also know that the practice by global corporations of shifting profits around the planet to no- or low-tax jurisdictions is increasing. A March 2017 report estimates that US Fortune 500 companies held an estimated $2.6 trillion off-shore, avoiding $767 billion in US taxes each year.[35]

Another tool for wealthy individuals working to avoid taxation and oversight consists of complicated trusts that mask the real owners and beneficiaries of assets. These trust and tax avoidance techniques have a mind-numbing complexity for a purpose. They are designed to be opaque, difficult to trace, and shrouded in secrecy. Coupled with off-shore centers, these are the mechanisms that facilitate trillions of dollars to be shifted around the world and between family members.

One example of a trust mechanism that has enabled wealthy US nationals to avoid taxation is called a Granter Retained Annuity Trust (GRAT). Casino magnate Sheldon Adelson avoided paying $2.8 billion in US estate and gift taxes by shifting almost $8 billion to heirs using a set of 30 GRAT trusts. Hundreds of executives have used the technique, according to Securities and Exchange Commission filings, including Facebook founder Mark Zuckerberg, fashion designer Ralph Lauren,

DISH Network chairman Charles Ergen, and 84 current and former partners from Goldman Sachs, including CEO Lloyd Blankfein. JPMorgan Chase & Co. has so many clients that use GRAT trusts that they have a special unit of the bank devoted to processing GRAT paperwork. The creator of the trust estimates it has cost the US Treasury at least $100 billion in lost revenue.[36]

Until now, our discussion of inequality has focused on policy drivers, such as low wages and tax policies, and the responsibility of elected officials in shaping a system of rules and policies. But there are also unelected actors who play a significant role in shaping this system: professional wealth managers.

Without the professional foot soldiers of the "wealth defense industry," our communities and countries would not lose trillions to trusts and off-shore shelters. These individual wealth managers, estate planners, tax lawyers, accountants, and trustees are the architects of off-shore subsidiaries, complex trusts, and other mechanisms that mask ownership and hide wealth. Without their work, tax avoidance would not exist on the global scale that it does today.

On the corporate side, teams of tax lawyers and accountants add nothing to the efficiency of markets or the quality of products. A growing number of corporations, such as General Electric, view their tax accounting departments as profit centers. Instead of building a better consumer product or service, these companies invest in designing a better tax scam.[37]

"The off shore system requires expertise to understand the tax systems of foreign lands and which institutions to trust," says Brooke Harrington, an expert on wealth management and author of *Capital without Borders: Wealth Management and the One Percent.* "A wealth manager must learn not just to work in one country like the Cayman Islands or Switzerland or the Cook Islands. They are managing wealth in a whole global ecosystem that is orchestrated by wealth managers who often write the laws in these places. It's a complex instrument or machine that only they know how to operate."[38]

The primary task of wealth managers, Harrington explains, is to "detach assets from states that wish to tax and regulate them, creating a form of capital that is, like its owners, 'transnational' and 'hypermobile.'" By artificially manipulating transactions of money across borders, wealth managers create not only asset-holding and tax avoidance structures, but a new body of transnational institutions that are expanding beyond the reach of any democratic accountability and oversight. The rise of off-shore centers would not happen without the lubrication provided by these wealth defense enablers.[39]

Wealthy families retain professional services or create "family offices" to manage and protect wealth, and ensure its transfer to future generations. The House of Morgan and John D. Rockefeller pioneered the first family offices in the US by bringing professional investment services, estate planning, and philanthropic activities all under one family-owned roof. The number of family offices has increased dramatically over the last two decades, corresponding with the rise of the super-rich. On the global level, there are now more than 10,000 family offices serving families that possess assets over $200 million each. More than half of these family offices have been founded since 2000. An estimated 1,000 family offices are based in London alone, managing over $1 trillion in private wealth.[40] With an estimated $16 trillion transferring within ultra-high net worth families over the next 30 years, the appetite for such family offices will increase.

A central activity of these offices is tax planning and reduction. This may involve the use of foreign shell corporations, opaque family trusts, foreign bank accounts, and financial planning techniques to convert one type of income (wage earnings) into another type (capital or royalty income) that may be taxed at a lower rate.

Fixing the Hidden Wealth Problem

Dismantling the off-shore system will require legislative action, international diplomacy, and sanctions and penalties aimed at banks, tax haven jurisdictions, and the wealth defense industry professions that facilitate the process. Wealth managers and family offices will contend they are just "helping families" and "obeying the laws" while helping shape the rules that govern wealth transmission and undermine enforcement.

The US has enormous responsibility and leverage in fixing this broken system, given the nation's oversized role in the global economy. The US should require transparency reforms and shared reporting as part of international trade agreements. Foreign banks and corporations should be held to higher standards of reporting in order to have access to US markets.

As part of global trade negotiations, countries should establish treaties requiring uniform disclosure and transparency, both of banks and capital flows. One piece of proposed legislation, the

Incorporation Transparency and Law Enforcement Assistance Act, would require all US companies, with few exceptions, to disclose the actual names of those who own or control them when they are formed, and to keep that information updated.[41] Private bank accounts should be required to disclose ownership of different accounts. And states like Delaware and Wyoming should have higher transparency and disclosure requirements for incorporation.

Some of the policy actions that would greatly reduce tax haven abuses include a global registry of beneficial ownership. International treaties should require banks and corporations to register their beneficial owners, ending one of the hallmarks of secrecy in the off-shore system. More than 300 economists called on the UK to take leadership in pushing this transparency reform, given its unique position as having "sovereignty over around a third of the world's tax havens."[42]

One legislative proposal, introduced by Senator Sheldon Whitehouse and Rep. Lloyd Doggett, the Stop Tax Haven Abuse Act (S. 851), is an omnibus bill that would close a number of loopholes and empower the Internal Revenue Service (IRS) to identify and close foreign tax shelters.[43] Such reforms would shine a light on the off-shore systems of hidden wealth and crack down on some of the most widespread abuses. Most of these provisions would generate substantial revenue – worth altogether over $100 billion a year – by ending the international shell game that corporations play.

Certain practices and trusts should simply be outlawed. Individuals use and abuse many of the same mechanisms as global corporations. While respecting principles of privacy, certain practices that are deliberately designed to mask ownership of wealth, bank accounts, corporations, and transactions must be declared illegal – along with the intent to design new loopholes that have yet to be discovered. Corporate shell structures and trust mechanisms that serve no purpose other than to obfuscate ownership and avoid taxation should be outlawed. Under estate tax reform proposals, the GRAT proposal described above should be prohibited. Unfortunately, the wealth defense industry is usually two steps ahead of the politicians when it comes to creating artful dodges.

One approach is to focus on holding the wealth defense practitioners directly responsible for aggressive tax avoidance, including criminal charges for aiding and abetting services. Sociologist Brooke Harrington observed: "The Israeli government was savvy. They figured out who the real adversary was

– the wealth management industry – and they targeted the enablers. Without the legal and accounting advice, people wouldn't be taking money out of the country." Harrington describes how the Israeli government approached three leading professionals and enlisted their assistance in closing loopholes concerning taxation and expatriation of wealth. Israel has turned wealth managers into compliance officers, not accessories to capital flight. Harrington believes greater pressure on professional associations would have an impact, including public shaming.[44]

To reverse inequality, the mountains of private wealth will need to be carved down to democratic size. But if private wealth is hidden, squirreled away in dynastic trusts, the job will be much harder. Fortunately, these pressure points are effective starting points.

5

Transformative Campaigns to Change the Future

Many US voters are skeptical about government being able to play a meaningful role in reducing inequality and improving the prospects for working people. We have lost sight of the ways that together – acting through government – we have undertaken what investment banker Felix Rohatyn calls "bold endeavors" to build infrastructure, opportunity, and an educated citizenry.[1]

In a time of diminished vision, it is inspiring to reflect on such undertakings as the construction of the Eire canal, the intercontinental railroad system, expanded rural electrification, and the Reconstruction Finance Corporation during the 1930s Great Depression. In the years after the Civil War, the Land Grant Colleges provided the foundation for improved agricultural practices and the modern state university systems. In the decades after

World War Two, the US built an interstate highway system, put astronauts on the moon, and expanded homeownership and access to higher education for millions of households.

Most people believe that Social Security in the US came about during the 1930s because of President Franklin D. Roosevelt. The real history is a powerful grassroots movement, propelled by an idea called the "Townsend Plan," which created the national constituency for Social Security. In 1933, Dr. Frances Townsend wrote an op-ed for a Long Beach, California newspaper, outlining the need for a national old age pension plan. The original concept, in the context of the depression, was to provide pensions to older workers so they could retire, opening up jobs in the labor market for younger workers. Funds were to be spent in the month they were received in order to have a stimulative impact on local economies.

This idea went viral, sparking interest from across the country. Within two years, there were clubs in every congressional district in the country pressing for the Townsend Plan. This transformative campaign led to the passage of the Social Security Act that dramatically reduced poverty amongst the elderly in the US and enabled millions of seniors and those with special needs to live decent lives.

Imagine a similar campaign today, with students from every college and university (and their parents) organizing lobbying committees in every congressional district. Their demand would be a debt-free college education fund, capitalized by a tax on substantial wealth. Such a movement – with 44 million potential constituents – would have the power to remove intransigent elected officials who are subservient to the college-debt industry.

Our poverty of imagination has been accompanied by a phony fiscal austerity, as taxes for the wealthy have been reduced and wealth is hidden. This has led to deep disinvestment. "The national is falling apart – literally," observes Rohatyn. "America's roads and bridges, schools and hospitals, airports and roadways, ports and dams, water lines and air control systems – the country's entire infrastructure is rapidly and dangerously deteriorating."[2]

Four Transformative Campaigns

Putting forward big ideas that spark the public imagination – and engaging constituencies to work for them – is how we overcome these barriers. For a campaign to be "transformative," it must do four things:

- put forward a bold endeavor that engages a large constituency of people to fight for and defend the policy;
- expand jobs and opportunities for those excluded from prosperity in the current unequal economy;
- reduce the concentration of wealth and power – often generating tax revenue to pay for the transformative program;
- rewire the drivers of inequality, reforming the most destructive dimensions of extractive capitalism.

What follows are four examples of "transformative" campaigns that advance monumental changes that would greatly improve the quality of people's lives, engage constituencies, reduce the power of concentrated wealth, and simultaneously address systemic drivers of inequality.

Everyone Gets a Home Before Government Subsidizes Second Homes

As any affluent family can attest, wealth matters. Wealth enables families to weather financial storms and provide a cushion against adversity.

Assets contribute to multi-generational well-being as families provide private safety nets and "transmit advantage" to children and grandchildren. The financial literacy book and board game, *Rich Dad, Poor Dad*, teaches people how to get on the positive net worth side of life through saving, purchasing a home, investing, and taking advantage of the wide range of tax incentives for wealth-building.

One transformative campaign would aim to reverse upside-down subsidies to expand homeownership and wealth for those excluded by lack of opportunity. The federal government provides hundreds of billions of dollars a year to individuals and families to build private wealth. This help, however, does not come in the form of direct cash outlays, but rather in the form of tax breaks. While this form of "back door" spending is less understood, policymakers all agree that it is a form of government spending, or a "tax expenditure."

In 2013, the federal government spent over $540 billion to assist private individuals build wealth. This took the form of tax incentives for homeownership, retirement, higher education, and savings. These programs, however, are completely "upside-down" in terms of who benefits. Most of these tax subsidies do not go to those who need them the most. Instead, the overwhelming bulk of these billions go to the "already have a lot," the richest 5 percent of households.[3]

Without appropriating any new funds, these subsidy programs could be dramatically reoriented and directed to people who have been excluded from wealth-building and opportunity – as well as precarious middle-class families who have few savings. Such a change would require a political movement to challenge unnecessary subsidies for the wealthy, capping or eliminating subsidies to those with wealth over $500,000.

As discussed, homeownership in the US has been steadily declining since 2004. This is doubly troubling because home equity represents 70 percent of the wealth of low- and middle-income families. Even after the battering of the 2008 economic meltdown, millions of Americans aspire to homeownership and believe it is a viable route to wealth-building.

In 2015, the US government provided $211 billion in tax subsidies for homeownership, incentives that primarily went to the already wealthy to encourage them to buy bigger houses and take on additional mortgage debt. In contrast, the direct cash outlay budget for federal affordable housing programs is $55 billion.[4]

Two homeownership subsidies are the most regressive in terms of who benefits – and the ripest candidates for reform. They are the Mortgage Interest Deduction and the Real Estate Tax Deduction and they account for over $100 billion a year in tax expenditures. Shifting the beneficiaries of these tax subsidies would make a huge difference in the lives of millions of people.

The Mortgage Interest Deduction costs over $70 billion a year. Beneficiaries deduct interest from both their primary home and a second home. Married homeowners can deduct the first $1 million in mortgage *interest* (individuals can claim up to $500,000). The Real Estate Tax Deduction allows homeowners to deduct state and local taxes paid on owner-occupied homes.

The top 20 percent of income earners, mostly living in affluent communities, are the biggest beneficiaries of both these tax subsidies. This top one-fifth receive 72 percent of the value of the Mortgage Interest Deduction (worth $59.5 billion) and 70 percent of the Real Estate Tax Deduction ($20.4 billion). The richest 5 percent of households received more from these subsidies than the bottom 80 percent of households combined.

In contrast, the average benefit for a middle-income household with an annual income of $59,000 is $260. Both programs claim to expand homeownership, yet do almost nothing for households in the bottom one-fifth of income earners, who receive an average benefit of $3. By comparison, the average benefit for households in the top 0.1 percent is $17,276.

A basic principle of government policy and subsidies should be "let's help everyone buy a home before we help the wealthy buy a second home." US lawmakers should create a First-Time Homeowners loan program that is similar to the one that enabled white families to buy houses after World War Two. It should be paid for by reforming the current "upside-down" subsidy program. Congress should redesign the Mortgage Interest Deduction and the Real Estate Tax Deduction to cap their benefits and reduce the expenditure. Eliminating tax breaks flowing to the top 20 percent of households would allow for a reallocation of an estimated $80 billion. These funds should be targeted in the form of both tax breaks and direct expenditures to first time homebuyers, including those who lost homes due to predatory mortgage lending practices.

In addition to housing, we should assist families to build wealth by reversing upside-down savings and retirement subsidies. As with subsidies for homeownership, government policies to encourage savings and retirement are heavily skewed to the wealthy. At a time when a troubling number of US households have zero or negative wealth, limited public resources should not be focused on boosting the wealth of those with a lot.

An estimated 44 percent of households have less than 3 months' worth of financial reserves to survive, even if they drop their standard of living to poverty level. According to the Asset Scorecard, almost half of households are "liquid asset poor." And the median household wealth has been stalled for decades. In 2013, the median wealth in the US is $81,000.[5] Half of households have no retirement savings. And among households that do have retirement savings, the median amount is $40,000, insufficient for retirees to maintain anything close to their standard of living.[6]

Government wealth-building programs should be designed to change these metrics, to reduce the number of "liquid asset poor" households and boost the median household wealth. Unfortunately, the way in which we currently spend an estimated $170 billion in tax expenditures makes the inequality situation worse.

There are several ways to boost retirement savings by creating simple, safe, and affordable programs for low-wealth families. Such programs would have the additional benefit of reducing racial wealth disparities. The average black and Latino families today have more than $100,000 *less* in retirement savings than the average white family. One reason for this is that families of color have less access to employer-based retirement programs.[7]

In 2015, the US Treasury Department launched myRA, a program aimed at helping lower- and middle-income households build retirement security. It has already demonstrated impressive results. Initial research indicates it has the potential to close the racial wealth divide by as much as 5–7 percent.[8] To build on the success of the myRA program, the Savers Credit should be refundable, making it more accessible and advantageous to lower-wage earning households.

A Children's Savings Account (CSA) should be automatically opened at birth, ensuring that every child starts off with a small nest egg for their future. CSAs, sometimes called "baby bonds," are long-term asset-building accounts that grow over the life of a child. They are often seeded by an initial deposit and grow over time with family contributions and matching savings programs. At age 18, an account holder can begin to draw down on these accounts, usually for higher education or as capital for a small enterprise. Two members of Congress, Rep. Keith Ellison (D-MN) and Rep. Joe Crowley (D-NY) introduced USAccounts: Investing in America's

Future Action, which create universal CSAs and provide the initial $500 deposit. These programs should be funded by capping tax-supported retirement accounts above $1 million and redirecting funds to support refundable credits and programs targeted to wealth-building for those excluded.

By rewiring the subsidy system and mobilizing those without homeownership and wealth, we could build a movement to reverse this system of upside-down wealth-building subsidies and reallocate funds for those who truly need them.

Debt Free Higher Education for All, Funded by Wealth Taxation

A second transformative campaign is to reduce or eliminate student debt with federal and state taxes on high levels of wealth. Such a campaign would engage a potentially powerful constituency: college students, graduates, and their parents. It would reduce the concentration of wealth and funnel revenue to an investment that clearly expands opportunity for millions of people.

As inequality has grown, so has the explosion in college student debt. In 2016, seven in ten graduating college seniors took on some form of student debt, averaging $37,000.[9] More than 44 million households hold some form of student debt. Total US student debt is approaching $1.4 trillion, surpassing auto loans and credit card debt and closing in on total mortgage debt.

The average monthly student loan repayment for borrowers between the ages of 20 and 30 is $351. For someone earning the minimum wage, that's 48 hours of work per month just for the loan, never mind shelter and food. This explains why the formal delinquency rate is 11.2 percent. Over 43 percent of borrowers – together owing $200 billion – have either stopped making payments or are behind on their student loans.[10]

Contrast this picture with the decades between 1945 and 1975 when millions of people attended college with little or no debt. Tuition at some of the flagship higher education systems in the country was close to zero, including the land grant universities.

The negative repercussions of student debt ripple through private lives and public trends. Indebted graduates begin their post-college work lives with high economic vulnerability and damaged credit histories. Young debt holders are less inclined to engage in entrepreneurship or take lower-salaried public interest work.[11] They delay forming families and purchasing homes, slowing positive asset formation.[12] The only winners in this system are the financial industry and loan serving agencies with their wide array of complicated loan products.

The student debt crisis of the last 15 years is rooted in the decline of state and federal spending on higher education. Many states slashed higher education funding in the aftermath of the 2008 economic meltdown. And while some states have since restored lost funding, spending on two- and four-year public college courses is still $10 billion below pre-recession levels, adjusted for inflation. In all, 46 states are spending less than they did prior to the recession; Montana, North Dakota, Wisconsin, and Wyoming are the exceptions. These 46 states are spending 18 percent less per student – and 9 states have cut higher education investment by 30 percent.[13]

Tax cuts for the wealthy have contributed to this decline in public investment in higher education. Starting in 2005, as was discussed earlier, 32 states lost their state-level estate taxes, a levy paid only by multi-millionaires and billionaires. This loss of $3–$6 billion a year created a huge hole in many state budgets, leading directly to higher education cuts.[14] Since 2008, average tuition has increased by more than $3,500 for four-year courses at public colleges and universities in these states. Florida, meanwhile, lost $700 million a year – and raised tuition fees by nearly $2,500. Michigan lost $155 million a year and hiked average tuition fees up by $2,200.[15]

There are a number of sources of revenue that could finance a debt-free tuition program and have the added benefit of reducing the concentration of wealth. Many are politically unpopular – due to protracted campaigns by wealthy interests to eliminate them. So linking the revenue to a mobilized constituency of students and their parents would politically protect the taxes. In Washington state, an estate tax only paid by millionaires is dedicated to an "education legacy trust fund" that supports K-12 education and state higher education. In 2006, anti-tax forces put forward a ballot initiative to eliminate the tax. But 62 percent of voters in the state supported retaining it, demonstrating the power of dedicating the revenue to a public good that has a constituency to defend it.[16]

The Washington state program could be replicated in other states by restoring estate taxes and dedicating revenue to tuition-free education programs. There are 32 states that lost their state-level estate taxes after 2005. They could all restore these taxes and dedicate the revenue to low or no tuition programs, starting in their public state and university education systems.

A federal version of a "state-level student opportunity fund" could be capitalized by a number of sources. Bill Gates, Sr., the father of the founder of Microsoft, received the education benefits of the GI Bill after World War Two. This enabled him to attend both college and law school at the University of Washington. He has called for a "GI Bill for the next generation," providing college tuition grants to any young person who completes two years of national service, civilian or military.[17]

As a stepping stone to tuition-free higher education, the College for All Act was introduced into Congress in April 2017 to lower student interest rates for new undergraduate borrowers and cap interest rates at 5 percent for undergraduate students and 8.25 percent for graduate students. Existing borrowers would be able to refinance their loans at these lower rates. The legislation fleshes out the Pell Grant program and expands uses to include housing and transportation. It triples current funding levels for federal work–study programs to enable the participation of an additional 1.4 million students.[18] The College for All program would be paid for by a Wall Street financial speculation and transaction tax that would raise $600 billion over 10 years. The tax would impose a financial transaction tax of 0.5 percent on stock trades, a 0.1

percent fee on bonds, and a 0.005 percent fee on derivatives.[19]

Even cities are getting engaged, tapping another source of revenue in the form of a municipal luxury real estate transaction tax. In 2016, San Francisco voters levied a real estate transfer tax on all properties in the city selling for $5 million or more. The measure is expected to raise $44 million a year, according to the *San Francisco Chronicle*. The city announced it will direct a portion of this revenue to provide free tuition and a $500 annual grant for textbooks and supplies to any San Francisco resident wishing to enroll at San Francisco City College. The free tuition program is available to anyone who has lived in the city for at least a year, regardless of income. "Even the children of the founders of Facebook," said city supervisor Jane Kim.[20]

Funding debt-free education with progressive taxes meets the criteria of a transformative campaign. A debt-free college program expands opportunities for those who have been excluded. By paying for it using a tax on inherited wealth, we reduce the concentration of wealth. These taxes have been hard to protect, in part because anti-tax groups have spent millions in order to save billions for wealthy families, in part by confusing the public over who actually pays the taxes.[21] By engaging students and their parents, we mobilize a powerful constituency to advocate for the policy and defend it in the future.

Save the Planet and Create Good Jobs

This transformative policy campaign would create millions of good jobs expanding our green infrastructure, funded by a carbon tax that would create incentives to reduce fossil fuel emissions.

US infrastructure is in substandard shape. The American Society of Civil Engineers gives a D+ grade for US infrastructure conditions, citing the failure to invest in critical maintenance and new initiatives such as public water works, transportation, bridges and roads, and energy facilities. This failure to address the $1.4 trillion national infrastructure spending gap by 2025 will result in a fall of $4 trillion in GDP, resulting in a loss of 2.5 million jobs.[22]

The US must address these deteriorating conditions, while also making a swift transition to a post-carbon economy with substantial infrastructure investments in retrofitting private homes and public buildings, smart electric grids, and decentralized renewable energy. According to scientists, the world cannot burn more than 20 percent of the existing carbon assets of oil, gas, and coal. To avert climate catastrophe, we must keep these fossil fuel assets in the ground.[23]

Investments in green infrastructure will generate millions of highly skilled jobs rooted in localities that cannot be outsourced. For this reason, public investment in infrastructure investment will revive aggregate consumer demand, alleviate inequality, and boost healthy growth both immediately and over the long term. Well-designed public infrastructure investments raise output in both the short and the longer term, according to an empirical study by the IMF.[24]

Funds to pay for such infrastructure investments should be linked to reducing extreme inequality and cutting carbon emission risks. One such mechanism is a targeted tax on the heaviest carbon users, which largely corresponds to the wealthiest households. Wealthy households have more carbon-intensive lifestyles, undertake more air travel, own multiple and larger homes and vehicles, and generally have much bigger carbon footprints.

A growing number of countries and US states understand the vital importance of putting a price on carbon to reduce fossil fuel consumption and facilitate the transition to a renewable green economy. Carbon taxes in British Columbia, Canada, and several European countries – including Denmark, Sweden, and Norway – provide market incentives to reduce consumption and shift investment to conservation and renewable energy.

A broad-based carbon tax could impose significant burdens on lower-income people, especially those in rural areas with long commutes for work and extended family. For this reason, some carbon tax proposals include per capita rebates – or dividends – to offset the increased cost of energy from fossil fuels. The US almost passed a version of a "cap and dividend" system in 2009 as part of comprehensive energy shift legislation. Unfortunately, the powerful fossil fuel lobby blocked this effort.

The shift to renewable energy systems will have a dislocating impact on communities that have traditionally benefitted from the fossil fuel sector, such as coal mining towns and regions of the country whose fortunes have been tied to oil and gas extraction and refineries. The transition to a post-carbon energy future will have winners and losers. To build political support for a timely transition requires a set of "just transition" policies so that no regions or individual workers carry a disproportionate burden of shifting away from fossil fuels.

A number of environmental and worker advocates have suggested the creation of "just transition funds" to smooth the move to renewable energy. Such a fund would include unemployment assistance for displaced workers, job retraining, and investment funds for new sustainable enterprises and businesses. Economist Robert Pollin calculates that such a fund would cost about $800 million a year. The fund could be expanded to provide ecological remediation to damaged communities and more substantial transition assistance to communities that have historically borne the costs of fossil fuel extraction, bringing the annual cost to $1.8 billion.[25]

One source of funds could be a luxury consumption tax on private jets, one of the most egregious sources of carbon pollution. There are more than 12,000 private luxury jets in the US and industry analysts project that over the next decade a further 9,000 new jets will be build, worth over $270 billion. They are owned and used by the most wealthy people on the planet. According to Wealth-X, the typical private jet owner is a 63-year-old male with a net worth of $1.6 billion. A luxury sales tax and an annual use fee on private jet ownership and use could generate substantial revenue.[26]

Carbon taxes and steep luxury taxes will be accused of dampening production and causing the elimination of jobs. This will be true for any initiative that shifts economic activity away from dependence on fossil fuels. In order to offset the negative impacts, funding for just transition programs are necessary. When such transition programs are in place, as in Germany, workers support energy transition initiatives.[27]

The US urgently needs to repair and adapt its existing infrastructure while reducing its dependence on fossil fuels. Investing in green jobs creates a constituency of workers and environmental activists who will be the political advocates and defenders of these programs. And taxing the carbon hogs and profligate consumers of existing natural resources is a fair and effective way to pay for it.

Universal Basic Income Funded by Commonwealth Funds

A growing number of thinkers and policy activists are exploring the potential of a "universal basic income" (UBI) or "guaranteed income." A renewed interest in a UBI is motivated by the prospects of increased automation and technological change reducing jobs and wage income opportunity. Others support a UBI because of the perceived failure of welfare programs to lift people out of poverty and the efficiency of direct cash assistance. There is a growing convergence that after several decades of stagnant wages and persistent poverty rates, a UBI could be an important boost to low incomes.

One living example of a universal basic income at a state level is the Alaska Permanent Fund, which captures a portion of the state's revenue from oil extracted from the publicly owned North Slope oil fields. The Fund issues an annual dividend to each resident of Alaska, ranging from $1,000 to $3,000 over the last several years. Children are eligible for the fund, so an annual dividend of $1,500 for a family of five would boost their yearly income by $7,500.[28]

One advocate of a UBI is Andy Stern, former president of the Service Employees International Union (SEIU), the country's biggest union, with 2.2 million members. Stern has spent the last decade looking at growing inequality, the polarization of jobs at the top and bottom of the wage scale, and the decline of labor force participation masked by declining unemployment rates. He has also examined technology's impact on jobs – not just robots – but the myriad ways that labor is being engineered out of enterprises. As Stern writes in *Raising the Floor*, his book advocating a UBI: "This job-less, wage-less growth isn't an aberration; nor is it temporary. It marks a strategic inflection point that merits our immediate and serious attention."

One UBI proposal is to phase in a $1,000 a month UBI for every adult starting at the age of 18. A couple would therefore have $24,000 per year, enough to lift them up out of poverty but not so much that they might quit working. This UBI plan would be a no-strings-attached cash grant, without work requirements or expectation of citizenship duties, such as being tied to national service.

There are other variations of UBI proposals, but most advocates support the principles of a universal cash grant, of simplicity, and of delinking UBI from efforts to address other civic and political objectives (like promoting voting or universal service).

There are a number of interesting experiments – for example, in Finland and in Oakland, California – where pilot schemes have introduced the concept of a UBI as a supplement to wage income.[29] In Ontario, Canada, the province is embarking on a three-year pilot project, providing a UBI to 4,000 low-income residents in three cities. Individuals will receive $12,500 a year, with couples receiving $17,600. While the UBI will be adjusted based on their wage income, recipients will continue to receive child or disability benefits, if applicable. "It's not an extravagant sum by any means," said Ontario's premier, Kathleen Wynne. "But our goal is clear. We want to find out whether a basic income makes a positive difference in people's lives. Whether this new approach gives them the ability to begin to achieve their potential."[30]

Critics of UBI worry that it will lead to mass laziness and a decline in productivity. In response, Stern writes: "A UBI at this level doesn't discourage people from working; it enables them to not take jobs that pay too little relative to the fulfillment they offer. Most people will want to keep working, because they aspire to a more comfortable lifestyle."[31] As one UBI supporter quipped, the basic income is enough to get you to the first floor. But if you want the better view from the seventh floor, you need to earn more money.

UBI has the potential to build a broad coalition of supporters across the political spectrum with a huge boost from a segment of Silicon Valley entrepreneurs who understand the societal costs of technological disruption. Supporters of a guaranteed income range from Martin Luther King, Jr. and Ralph Nader to libertarians like Charles Murray and Michael Tanner of the Cato Institute.

Libertarians view UBI as a way to free poor people from bureaucracies of inefficient and humiliating government welfare programs. They support "cashing out" the 126 anti-poverty programs that cost $1 trillion a year – such as food stamps, housing assistance, and the Earned Income Tax Credit – and redirecting funds to a UBI. Most libertarians would also like to eliminate all the federal government income transfer programs, including Social Security, Medicaid, and Medicare.

A UBI is not an excuse to dismantle an already weak US social safety net. Rather, a UBI should be designed both to "raise the floor" and also, through its financing mechanism, reduce the concentration of wealth and power.

The $1,000 a month UBI plan for every adult would cost between $1.75 and $2.5 trillion per year. The mechanism of paying for a UBI will determine whether it remains a safety net program or is transformational and reduces inequality. Not all supporters of UBI will stay on board if it addresses the bigger concern of structural inequality, but a significant constituency will remain.

Some revenue sources are provisions we've discussed earlier. For instance, eliminating tax expenditures could raise $1.2 trillion a year. These "upside-down subsidies" mostly benefit the very affluent who take deductions for mortgage interest, real estate taxes, investment expenses, charitable contributions, foreign taxes, interest on state and local bonds, etc.

A financial transaction tax could raise $150 billion a year toward a universal basic income. A modest levy on Wall Street transactions, a penny on every four dollars of stock, bond, and derivative transfers, could yield substantial annual funds that could be dedicated to a UBI. A modest 1.5 percent flat wealth tax levied on personal assets over $1 million would generate an estimated $600 billion.

One perspective, dating back to Thomas Paine, is to create an income stream from those assets we hold in common. UBI supporters like Peter Barnes point out that affluent households benefit from property income and rents from their ownership of assets. Shouldn't everyone, he argues, receive property income from resources that we theoretically co-inherited together, such as the atmosphere, the broadcast spectrum, and natural resources? Then, instead of giving these shared assets to corporations for free, we should charge rent and use fees, using the proceeds to pay dividends or a UBI to every American – one person, one share. A dividend tied to natural resources simultaneously supplements declining wage income and reduces our destruction of nature. Taxing consumers of the commons – including the dumping of carbon into the atmosphere – encourages better management of scarce natural resources and contributes to a reduction in inequality.

Technological change will bring further disruption to the workplace and continue to push wages down. As a result, there will be a growing constituency for a universal basic income and the base for a mass movement. But for a UBI to go beyond another "raise the floor" provision and benefit low-income people, it must add to our current safety net, not shrink it. It should tap the growing concentration of wealth, slicing it down to democratic size.

Conclusion:
Toward Equality

Inequality in America is reversible. The first order is to shift the economic trajectory away from a perilous course toward patrimonial capitalism and plutocracy.

More than 40 years of stagnant wages and wealth pooling at the top has fueled a populist rebellion, albeit confused as to who is responsible for the pain. A deeply polarized economy has given rise to a polarized politics that can either tip "progressive populist" or "regressive populist." This future is in our hands.

The good news is that there is broad recognition that the rules of the economy are rigged in favor of wealthy elites. To expand this understanding, we must educate the wider public about the causes and drivers of inequality, not the simplistic narratives and flawed theories of individual performance. The rules of the economy have been tipped in favor of asset owners at the expense of wage earners. These human-created rules can be fixed.

To reverse these inequalities will require transformative policy campaigns that project a bold vision of what we can do together. These efforts must ignite imaginations that have been dampened down and are suspicious of common endeavors.

The policy agenda described in this book – such as eliminating student debt, expanding good jobs through green infrastructure, establishing a universal basic income, and expanding homeownership and wealth-building opportunities – are examples of big interventions that will reverse inequality. They will help rewire the economy for equity and broadly shared prosperity.

To succeed, these campaigns must engage constituencies of people to press for change – and finance these programs in ways that reduce the distorting impact of concentrated wealth and power. Where opportunities are blocked by a political system captured by wealth and global corporations, we must act where there is agency and room to move. I personally would bet my retirement on the millennial generation emerging as a political force to reverse inequality. In the coming years, I predict the rising up of a progressive populist movement to eliminate student debt and expand economic opportunity.

In order to succeed, such movements will have to disrupt the societal stories and narratives that justify and hold inequalities in place. We must supplant individualistic stories of success with a wider recognition of the role of commonwealth in individual success and fortune. We must lift up stories of people who understand that a web of public investments unpins the existing commonwealth – and that it is the responsibility of the wealthy and of older generations to pay their taxes in order to protect and expand this commonwealth for future generations.

As our national stories and narratives shift – and we see the vibrant commonwealth that makes our lives possible – it will become clearer what to call those who privatize societal wealth for their individual gain. They are freeloaders and looters – and we must defend our communities from their selfish reach.

After reading this book, some readers may still feel wary of proposals that redistribute wealth and power, concerned that such actions will reduce the dynamism of the economy, undermine freedom, and lead us down a modern day "road to serfdom." What these doubters ignore is that the present day extremes of wealth and power – and their future trajectory – are propelling us toward a society that none of us, including the wealthy, will want to live in. Festering inequalities are destroying our society's healthy foundations, sowing toxic seeds of instability, social breakdown, and economic volatility. Anyone concerned about freedom and economic health should be leading the parade to reverse inequality.

A more equitable society will unleash positive possibilities and human potential, lifting up the talents and gifts of millions of people locked into poverty and economic insecurity. As Sam Pizzigati writes in *Greed and Good*: "If we want to lead longer lives, if we want more time in these lives for those we love and the work we love to do, if we want our society to have the wherewithal – and the will – to address the challenges we see all around us, we need to narrow the gap that separates the wealthy from everyone else."[1]

Reversing inequality is not only possible. It is the only path forward.

Notes

Introduction

1 Thomas Piketty, Emmanuel Saez, and Gabriel Zucman, *Distributional National Accounts: Methods and Estimates for the United States.* National Bureau of Economic Research Working Paper No. 22945. December 2016. http://www.nber.org/papers/w22945.

2 Kelley Phillips Erb, "Portland Plans to Tax Companies Who Pay CEOs 100 Times More than Workers," *Forbes*, December 19, 2016. http://www.forbes.com/sites/kellyphillipserb/2016/12/19/portland-plans-to-tax-companies-who-pay-ceos-100-times-more-than-workers/#211ff3dc5240.

3 Lawrence Mishel and Alyssa Davis, "Top CEOs Make 300 Times More than Typical Workers," Economic Policy Institute, June 21, 2015. http://www.epi.org/publication/top-ceos-make-300-times-more-than-workers-pay-growth-surpasses-market-gains-and-the-rest-of-the-0-1-percent/.

4 Thomas Piketty and Emanuel Saez, "Income Inequality in the United States, 1913–1998," *Quarterly Journal of Economics*, 118/1, 2003, pp. 1–39, Tables A3 and A6. Updated version downloaded from http://eml. berkeley.edu/~saez/. Figures are in real 2013 dollars and include capital gains. These figures have been updated for 2009–14 by Piketty and Saez.

5 Edward Wolff, "Trends in Household Wealth in the United States, 1962–83 and 1983–89," *Review of Income and Wealth*, 40/2, June 1994, p. 153. http:// piketty.pse.ens.fr/files/WolffRIW1994.pdf.

6 Chuck Collins and Josh Hoxie, "Billionaire Bonanza: The Forbes 400 and the Rest of US," Institute for Policy Studies, December 2015. http://www.ips-dc. org/billionaire-bonanza/.

7 Prosperity Now, "On Track or Left Behind: Findings from the 2017 Prosperity Now Scorecard," July 2017, p. 6. https://scorecard.prosperitynow.org/find ings.

8 Rakesh Kochhar and Richard Fry, "Wealth Inequality Has Widened Along Racial, Ethnic Lines Since End of Great Recession," Pew Research Center, December 12, 2014. http://www.pewresearch.org/fact-tank/ 2014/12/12/racial-wealth-gaps-great-recession/.

9 Chuck Collins, Dedrick Asante-Muhammed, Emanuel Nieves, Josh Hoxie, "Ever-Growing Gap," Institute for Policy Studies and Corporation for Enterprise Development, August 2016. https://www. ips-dc.org/report-ever-growing-gap/.

10 See Sam Pizzigati, *The Rich Don't Always Win*. Seven Stories Press, 2012.

Chapter 1: Why Does Inequality Matter? (And Why Is It Happening?)

1 Chuck Collins, Dedrick Asante-Muhammed, Emanuel Nieves, Josh Hoxie, "Ever-Growing Gap," Institute for Policy Studies and Corporation for Enterprise Development, August 2016. https://www.ips-dc.org/report-ever-growing-gap/.

2 For a good overview of health and inequality issues, see Sam Pizzigati, *Greed and Good: Understanding and Overcoming the Inequality That Limits Our Lives.* Apex Press, 2004, pp. 311–330. Also see Dr. Stephen Bezruchka's website, Population Health Forum, at http://depts.washington.edu/eqhlth/, for information on global and US health and inequality information.

3 Stephen Bezruchka, "Inequality Kills," *Boston Review*, April 2, 2014. http://bostonreview.net/us/stephen-bezruchka-inequality-kills.

4 Also see US Institute of Medicine, *US Health in International Perspective: Shorter Lives, Poorer Health.* National Academies Press, 2013. https://www.ncbi.nlm.nih.gov/pubmed/24006554.

5 Joshua Holland, "High Inequality Results in More US Deaths than Tobacco, Car Crashes and Guns Combined," *Moyers*, April 19, 2014. http://billmoyers.com/2014/04/19/high-inequality-results-in-more-us-deaths-than-tobacco-car-crashes-and-guns-combined/#.VY1GJPrs9dk.twitter. This parallels the results of the Columbia University study on deaths due to poverty, segregation, lack of education, etc. These are correlative in the USA with the inequality

coefficient. Both studies arrive at around 875,000 deaths per year. See http://www.mailman.columbia.edu/academic-departments/epidemiology/research-service/death-poverty.

6 Anne Case and Angus Deaton, "Mortality and Morbidity in the 21st Century," Brookings Institution, March 23, 2017. https://www.brookings.edu/bpea-articles/mortality-and-morbidity-in-the-21st-century/.

7 Daniel Sage, "Are More Equal Societies the Most Cohesive? A Cross-National Study into Income Inequality and Social Cohesion," School of Applied Social Science, University of Stirling, 2012, p. 3. http://www.social-policy.org.uk/lincoln2012/Sage%20P4.pdf.

8 Sean F. Reardon and Kendra Bischoff, "Growth in the Residential Segregation of Families by Income, 1970–2009," *Stanford University*, US 2010 Project, Russell Sage Foundation and American Communities Project at Brown University, November 2011. http://www.s4.brown.edu/us2010/Data/Report/report111111.pdf.

9 Richard Wilkinson, *Unhealthy Societies: The Afflictions of Inequality*. Routledge, 1997, p. 4.

10 Robert Putnam, *Bowling Alone*. Simon & Schuster, 2000.

11 M. Islam, J. Merlo, I. Kawachi, M. Lindström, and U. Gerdtham, "Social Capital and Health: Does Egalitarianism Matter? A Literature Review," *International Journal for Equity in Health*, 5/3, 2006, p. 6.

12 Daniel Sage, "Are More Equal Societies the Most Cohesive? A Cross-National Study into Income

Inequality and Social Cohesion," School of Applied Social Science, University of Stirling, 2012, p. 13. http://www.social-policy.org.uk/lincoln2012/Sage%20P4.pdf.

13 OECD, "A Family Affair: Intergenerational Social Mobility across OECD Countries," *Economic Policy Reforms, Going for Growth*.https://www.oecd.org/eco/public-finance/chapter%205%20gfg%202010.pdf. Also see the Pew Charitable Trust's Economic Mobility Project (www.economicmobility.org) and their study, "Chasing the Same Dream, Climbing Different Ladders: Economic Mobility in the United States and Canada," Economic Mobility Project, January 2010. http://www.pewtrusts.org/~/media/legacy/uploadedfiles/pcs_assets/2010/pewempuscanadapdf.pdf.

14 Raj Chetty, David Grusky, Maximilian Hell, Nathaniel Hendren, Robert Manduca, and Jimmy Narang, "The Fading American Dream: Trends in Absolute Income Mobility Since 1940," *Science*, April 24, 2017. http://science.sciencemag.org/content/sci/early/2017/04/21/science.aal4617.full.pdf.

15 "Few Rewards: An Agenda to Give America's Working Poor a Raise," Economic Policy Institute and Oxfam America, June 22, 2016. https://www.oxfamamerica.org/explore/research-publications/few-rewards/.

16 See "President Jimmy Carter: The United States is an Oligarchy," YouTube Video, The Thom Hartmann Program, posted July 28, 2015. https://www.youtube.com/watch?t=16&v=hDsPWmioSHg.

17 Nicholas Confessore, Sarah Cohen, and Karen

Yourish, "Just 158 Families Have Provided Nearly Half of the Early Money for Efforts to Capture the White House," *New York Times*, October 15, 2015. https://www.nytimes.com/interactive/2015/10/11/us/politics/2016-presidential-election-super-pac-donors.html.

18 Jane Mayer, *Dark Money: The Hidden History of the Billionaires Behind the Rise of the Radical Right.* Doubleday, 2016.

19 Arthur Okun, *Equality and Efficiency: The Big Tradeoff.* Brookings Institution Press, May 1, 1975. https://www.brookings.edu/book/equality-and-efficiency/.

20 Joseph Stiglitz, "Inequality and Economic Growth," in Mariana Mazzucato and Michael Jacobs, eds., *Rethinking Capitalism: Economics and Policy for Sustainable and Inclusive Growth.* Wiley, 2016. https://www8.gsb.columbia.edu/faculty/jstiglitz/sites/jstiglitz/files/Inequality%20and%20Economic%20Growth_0.pdf.

21 K.E. Dynan, J. Skinner, and S.P. Zeldes, "Do the Rich Save More?" *Journal of Political Economy*, 112/2, 2004, pp. 397–444.

22 Raghuram G. Rajan, *Fault Lines: How Hidden Fractures Still Threaten the World Economy.* Princeton University Press, 2010.

23 David Lynch, "How Inequality Hurts the Economy," *Business Week Insider*, November 16, 2011. http://www.businessweek.com/magazine/how-inequality-hurts-the-economy-11162011.html?campaign_id=rss_topStories. Also see Andrew Berg and Jonathan D. Ostry, "Inequality and Unsustainable Growth: Two

Sides of the Same Coin?" IMF Staff Discussion Note, April 8, 2011.

24 R.A., "How Inequality Affects Growth," *The Economist*, June 15, 2015.

25 F. Cingano, "Trends in Income Inequality and Its Impact on Economic Growth," OECD Social, Employment and Migration Working Papers, No. 163, December 2014.

26 US Census Bureau, *Quarterly Homeownership Rates by Race and Ethnicity of Householder, 1994 to Present*, Table 16. https://www.census.gov/housing/hvs/data/histtabs.html. Quarterly updates are available at: http://www.census.gov/housing/hvs/files/cur renthvspress.pdf.

27 See the comments of Paul Graham, founder of Y Combinator. Sara Ashley O'Brien, "This Tech Investor Calls Himself a 'Manufacturer of Income Inequality'." http://money.cnn.com/2016/01/04/technology/y-com binator-paul-graham-income-inequality/.

28 Anthony B. Atkinson, *Inequality: What Can Be Done?* Harvard University Press, 2015; quoted in Robert Kuttner, "The New Inequality Debate," *The American Prospect*, January 14, 2016. http://pros pect.org/article/new-inequality-debate-0.

29 Historical data on union density at Gerald Mayer, *Union Membership Trends in the United States*, Congressional Research Service, August 31, 2004. http://digitalcommons.ilr.cornell.edu/cgi/viewcont ent.cgi?article=1176&context=key_workplace&sei-r edir=1#search=%22historical%20union%20membe rship%201950%22. Currently, almost 11 percent of

workers are members of a union and close to 12 percent are covered by a collective bargaining agreement. See Barry T. Hirsch and David A. Macpherson, "Union Membership and Coverage Database from the Current Population Survey," at: http://www.unionstats.com/.

30 Andy Stern with Lee Kravitz, *Raising the Floor: How a Universal Basic Income Can Renew Our Economy and Rebuild the American Dream*. Public Affairs, 2016, p. 15.

31 Ben Bernanke, "The Level and Distribution of Economic Well-Being." Speech to the Greater Omaha Chamber of Commerce, February 7, 2007. https://www.federalreserve.gov/newsevents/speech/bernanke20070206a.htm.

32 Florence Jaumotte and Carolina Osorio Buitron, "Power from the People," *Finance & Development*, 52/1, International Monetary Fund, March 2015. http://www.imf.org/external/pubs/ft/fandd/2015/03/jaumotte.htm.

33 Thomas Piketty, Emmanuel Saez, and Gabriel Zucman, "Economic Growth in the United States: A Tale of Two Countries," Washington Center for Equitable Growth, blog post, December 6, 2016. http://equitablegrowth.org/research-analysis/economic-growth-in-the-united-states-a-tale-of-two-countries/.

Chapter 2: What Are the Barriers to Change?

1 David Daley, *Rat F**ked: Why Your Vote Doesn't Count*. Liveright Publishing, 2017 edn. with new epilogue, p. xxiv.

2 Leslie McCall, *The Undeserving Rich: American*

Beliefs about Inequality, Opportunity, and Redistribution. Cambridge University Press, 2013.

3 Chuck Collins, "Eight Lessons US Progressives Can Learn from the UK Labour Party," *Common Dreams*, July 26, 2017. https://www.commondreams.org/views/2017/07/26/eight-lessons-us-progressives-can-learn-uk-labour-party.

4 Miles Corak, "Economic Mobility," *Pathways*, special issue *State of the Union: The Poverty and Inequality Report 2016*, Stanford Center on Poverty and Inequality, pp. 51–57. http://inequality.stanford.edu/sites/default/files/Pathways-SOTU-2016.pdf.

5 Thomas Piketty, Emmanuel Saez, and Gabriel Zucman, *Distributional National Accounts: Methods and Estimates for the United States*. National Bureau of Economic Research Working Paper No. 22945. December 2016. http://www.nber.org/papers/w22945.

6 Malcolm Gladwell, *Outliers: The Story of Success*. Little, Brown and Company, 2008, pp. 33, 268.

Chapter 3: Changing the Rules: Raising Floors, Opening Doors

1 Stephen Bezruchka, "Inequality Kills," *Boston Review*, April 2, 2014. http://bostonreview.net/us/stephen-bezruchka-inequality-kills.

2 Kate Rogers, "Adjusted for Inflation, the Federal Minimum Wage is Worth Less than 50 Years Ago," *CNBC*, July 21, 2016. http://www.cnbc.com/2016/07/21/adjusted-for-inflation-the-federal-minimum-wage-is-worth-less-than-50-years-ago.html.

3 Jeanna Smialek, "Waitresses Stuck at $2.13 Hourly Minimum for 22 Years," *Businessweek*, April 23, 2013. https://www.bloomberg.com/news/articles/2013-04-25/waitresses-stuck-at-2-13-hourly-minimum-for-22-years.

4 National Conference of State Legislatures, "State Minimum Wages/2017 Minimum Wages by State." http://www.ncsl.org/research/labor-and-employment/state-minimum-wage-chart.aspx.

5 See these resources from the Labor Center at the University of California, Berkeley. http://laborcenter.berkeley.edu/minimum-wage-living-wage-resources/inventory-of-us-city-and-county-minimum-wage-ordinances/. And the National Employment Law Center. http://nelp.org/content/uploads/2015/03/LocalLivingWageOrdinancesandCoverage.pdf.

6 Henry J. Kaiser Family Foundation, "Key Facts about the Uninsured Population," September 29, 2016. http://kff.org/uninsured/fact-sheet/key-facts-about-the-uninsured-population/.

7 Laurel Avery, "We Must Demand Medicare for All," *Huffington Post*, March 13, 2017. http://www.huffingtonpost.com/entry/we-must-demand-medicare-for-all_us_58c6b690e4b0c3276fb78758.

8 Richard Reeves, *Dream Hoarders: How the American Upper Middle Class is Leaving Everyone Else in the Dust, Why That is a Problem, and What to Do About It*. Brookings Institution Press, 2017, pp. 11–12.

9 See information about the Arizona Redistricting Commission at: http://azredistricting.org and the

California Citizens Redistricting Commission: http://wedrawthelines.ca.gov.

10 Michael Wines, "Judges Find Wisconsin Redistricting Unfairly Favored Republicans," *New York Times*, November 21, 2016. https://www.nytimes.com/2016/11/21/us/wisconsin-redistricting-found-to-unfairly-favor-republicans.html?_r=0.

11 "The Fair Representation Act," FairVote. http://www.fairvote.org/fair_rep_in_congress#fair_rep_act.

12 Maine Commission on Governmental Ethics and Election Practices, "The Maine Clean Election Act." http://www.maine.gov/ethics/mcea/.

13 State Elections Enforcement Commission, "Citizens Election Program." http://www.ct.gov/seec/cwp/view.asp?a=3548&Q=489606.

14 Bill Turque, "Montgomery Council Approves Plan for Public Finance of Local Campaigns," *Washington Post*, September 30, 2014. https://www.washingtonpost.com/local/md-politics/montgomery-council-approves-plan-for-public-finance-of-local-campaigns/2014/09/30/b3e2b15c-482d-11e4-b72e-d60a9229cc10_story.html?tid=a_inl&utm_term=.2563297e03d2.

15 For statistics from this article and imbedded video piece, see Aly Chu, "Democracy Vouchers: Everything You Need to Know," *Crosscut,* March 3, 2017. http://crosscut.com/2017/03/democracy-vouchers-everything-you-need-to-know/.

16 For information about the Government By The People Act, see: https://www.congress.gov/bill/115th-congress/house-bill/20.

Chapter 4: Reducing the Concentration of Wealth

1 Jeffrey A. Winters, *Oligarchy*. Cambridge University Press, 2011, p. xiii.

2 See an excellent history: Kenneth Scheve and David Stasavage, *Taxing the Rich: A History of Fiscal Fairness in the United States and Europe*. Russell Sage Foundation, 2016.

3 Citizens for Tax Justice, "Who Pays Taxes in America in 2016?" April 12, 2016. http://www.ctj.org/who-pays-taxes-in-america-in-2016/.

4 See this IRS tax table: https://www.irs.gov/pub/irs-soi/12intop400.pdf. Also see: Noam Scheiber and Patricia Cohen, "For the Wealthiest, a Private Tax System that Saves Them Billions," *New York Times*, December 29, 2015. https://www.nytimes.com/2015/12/30/business/economy/for-the-wealthiest-private-tax-system-saves-them-billions.html?_r=1.

5 Buffett initially disclosed this information in an op-ed: "Stop Coddling the Super-Rich," *New York Times*, August 14, 2011. http://www.nytimes.com/2011/08/15/opinion/stop-coddling-the-super-rich.html. His effective tax rate subsequently went down from 17.4 percent to 16 percent. See Jeanne Sahadi, "Warren Buffett to Trump: 'I Have Paid Federal Income Taxes Every Year Since 1944'," *CNN Money*, October 10, 2016.

6 See this IRS table: https://www.irs.gov/businesses/small-businesses-self-employed/estate-tax.

7 Tax Policy Center, "Current Law Distribution of Gross Estate and Net Estate Tax by Size of Gross

Estate," 2013. http://www.taxpolicycenter.org/mod el-estimates/estate-tax-tables-2012/current-law-distri bution-gross-estate-and-net-estate-tax-3.

8 Roy Ulrich, "The Constitutionality of a Net Worth Tax," Goldman School of Public Policy, University of California, January 12, 2015. https://gspp.berkel ey.edu/news/news-center/the-constitutionality-of-a-net-worth-tax.

9 Roy Ulrich, "A Wealth Tax for the States," January 20, 2015. Available at SSRN: https://papers.ssrn. com/sol3/papers.cfm?abstract_id=2552968.

10 Teresa Ghilarducci, "Who is Finished Paying their 2017 Social Security Taxes?" *Huffington Post*, January 1, 2017. http://www.huffingtonpost.com/ teresa-ghilarducci/who-is-finished-paying-th_b_1392 4394.html.

11 Karen Smith, "Can Social Security Be Solvent?" Urban Institute, October 2015. http://www.urban.org/sites/ default/files/publication/72196/2015.10.16_How%2 0to%20make%20SS%20solvent_finalized.pdf.

12 "MEMO: Joint Tax Committee Finds Harkin, DeFazio Wall Street Trading and Speculators Tax Generates More Than $350 Billion," Office of Rep. Pete Defazio, November 9, 2011. http://defazio. house.gov/media-center/press-releases/memo-joint-tax-committee-finds-harkin-defazio-wall-street-tradi ng-and.

13 "The Inclusive Prosperity Act of 2017," Office of Senator Bernard Sanders. https://www.sanders. senate.gov/download/inclusive-prosperity-act-fact-sh eet?inline=file.

14 Robert Pollin, James Heintz, and Thomas Herndon, "The Revenue Potential of a Financial Transaction Tax for U.S. Financial Markets," Political Economic Research Institute, UMASS-Amherst, July 30, 2017. Working paper. https://www.peri.umass.edu/public ation/item/698-the-revenue-potential-of-a-financial-transaction-tax-for-u-s-financial-markets.

15 Leonard E. Burman, William G. Gale, Sarah Gault, Bryan Kim, James Nunns, and Steven M. Rosenthal, "Financial Transaction Taxes in Theory and Practice," Tax Policy Center, June 30, 2015. http://www.taxpolicycenter.org/publications/financial-tran saction-taxes-theory-and-practice.

16 Rick Wartzman, "Put a Cap on CEO Pay," *Business Week*, September 12, 2008. https://www.bloomberg. com/news/articles/2008-09-12/put-a-cap-on-ceo-paybusinessweek-business-news-stock-market-and-financial-advice.

17 For a review of the literature, check "The Ineffective Enterprise," a discussion that appears in Sam Pizzigati, *Greed and Good: Understanding and Overcoming the Inequality That Limits Our Lives.* Apex Press, 2004.

18 See congressional announcement from Senator Jack Reed. https://www.reed.senate.gov/news/releases/ reed-blumenthal-doggett-offer-bill-to-end-special-tax -exemptions-for-huge-ceo-bonuses.

19 Information about HR 6242 in 2016 congressional session is at: https://www.govtrack.us/congress/bills/ 114/hr6242.

20 City of Portland, "Executive Pay Ratio Business

Surtax," Revenue Division, Bureau of Revenue and Financial Services, Office of Management and Finance, April 2016. https://assets.documentcloud.org/documents/3039501/CEO-Charge.pdf.

21 Sharon Lee, "Inequality Battle Brewing at State-Level," *BNA Pension and Benefits Blog,* March 1, 2017. https://www.bna.com/income-inequality-battle-b57982084620/.

22 The Business Roundtable has identified the federal pay ratio disclosure rule as one of 16 top priority regulations for elimination – that's among *all* US regulations. See "Top Regulations of Concern," Business Roundtable, February 23, 2017. http://businessroundtable.org/top-regulations-concern.

23 "Whack-a-passenger," *The Economist*, April 22, 2017.

24 Bourree Lam, "2015: A Merger Bonanza," *The Atlantic,* January 9, 2016. https://www.theatlantic.com/business/archive/2016/01/2015-mergers-acquisitions/423096/.

25 Barry C. Lynn and Lina Kahn, "The Slow Motion Collapse of American Entrepreneurship," *Washington Monthly*, July/August 2012. http://washingtonmonthly.com/magazine/julyaugust-2012/the-slow-motion-collapse-of-american-entrepreneurship/. Barry Lynn, "Estates of Mind," *Washington Monthly*, July/August 2013. http://washingtonmonthly.com/magazine/julyaugust-2013/estates-of-mind/.

26 Gillian B. White, "How American Business Got So Big," *Atlantic Magazine*, November 18, 2016. https://www.theatlantic.com/business/archive/2016/11/trump-antitrust-barry-lynn/507917/.

27 Ben Potter, "How Seed Has Consolidated Since 2000," AgWeb blog, powered by *Farm Journal,* April 17, 2017. https://www.agweb.com/article/how-seed-has-consolidated-since-2000-naa-ben-potter/.

28 See Barry Lynn, *Cornered: The New Monopoly Capitalism and the Economics of Destruction.* Wiley, 2010.

29 Steven Davidoff, "Overhaul of Israel's Economy Offers Lessons for United States," *New York Times*, January 7, 2014. https://dealbook.nytimes.com/2014/01/07/overhaul-of-israels-economy-offers-lessons-for-united-states/?_r=1.

30 Chuck Collins, "The Panama Papers Expose the Hidden Wealth of the World's Super-Rich," *The Nation*, April 5, 2016. https://www.thenation.com/article/panama-papers-expose-the-hidden-wealth-of-the-worlds-super-rich/.

31 Michael Findley, Daniel L. Nielson, and Jason Sharman, *Global Shell Games: Experiments in Transnational Relations, Crime, and Terrorism.* Cambridge University Press, 2014. http://www.globalshellgames.com.

32 See Nicholas Shaxson, *Treasure Islands: Uncovering the Damage of Offshore Banking and Tax Havens.* Palgrave Macmillan, 2011.

33 Jesse Drucker summarizes the main points of Gabriel Zucman's *The Hidden Wealth of Nations: The Scourge of Tax Havens.* University of Chicago Press, 2015, at: http://www.bloomberg.com/news/articles/2015-09-21/if-you-see-a-little-piketty-in-this-tax-haven-book-that-s-fine.

34 Nicholas Confessore, "How to Hide $400 Million," *New York Times Magazine*, November 30, 2016. https://www.nytimes.com/2016/11/30/magazine/how-to-hide-400-million.html?_r=0.

35 Institute for Taxation and Economic Policy, "Fortune 500 Companies Hold a Record $2.6 Trillion Offshore," March 2017. http://itep.org/itep_reports/2017/03/fortune-500-companies-hold-a-record-26-trillion-offshore.php#.WQCJ6WV2TEw.

36 Zach Mider, "Accidental Tax Break Saves Wealthiest Americans $100 Billion," *Bloomberg News*, December 17, 2013. https://www.bloomberg.com/news/articles/2013-12-17/accidental-tax-break-saves-wealthiest-americans-100-billion.

37 David Kocieniewski, "G.E.'s Strategies Let It Avoid Taxes Altogether," *New York Times*, March 24, 2010. http://www.nytimes.com/2011/03/25/business/economy/25tax.html?_r=2.

38 Interview with Brooke Harrington, March 17, 2017.

39 Brooke Harrington, *Capital without Borders: Wealth Management and the One Percent.* Harvard University Press, 2016, p. 12.

40 David Batty, "How London's Booming 'Butler Class' Takes Care of the Wealthy Elite," *Guardian*, March 12, 2017. https://www.theguardian.com/business/2016/mar/12/family-office-private-wealth-funds.

41 See legislative summary for the Incorporation Transparency and Law Enforcement Assistance Act (HR 4450), introduced by Rep. Carolyn Maloney in the 114th Congress. https://www.congress.gov/bill/114th-congress/house-bill/4450. The Senate version,

introduced by Senator Sheldon Whitehouse in the 114th Congress (S-2489) largely mirrors the House version. https://www.congress.gov/bill/114th-congress/senate-bill/2489.

42 Henry Mance, "Economists Call for End of Tax Havens," *Financial Times*, May 8, 2016. https://www.ft.com/content/6464c7c0-1525-11e6-b197-a4af20d5575e.

43 A summary of the bill is available from Global Financial Integrity. http://www.gfintegrity.org/wp-content/uploads/2017/04/Stop-Tax-Haven-Abuse-Act-115th-summary-FINAL.pdf.

44 See Harrington, *Capital without Borders*. And interview, March 17, 2017.

Chapter 5: Transformative Campaigns to Change the Future

1 Felix Rohatyn, *Bold Endeavors: How Our Government Built America, and Why It Must Rebuild Now*. Simon & Schuster, 2009.

2 From a Business Visionaries Interview with Felix Rohatyn. See Stephanie Dahle, "Book Summary: Bold Endeavors," *Forbes*, March 24, 2009. https://www.forbes.com/2009/03/24/bold-endeavors-summary-opinions-business-visionaries-summary.html.

3 See Ezra Levin, Jeremie Greer, and Ida Rademacher, "From Upside Down to Right Side Up," Corporation for Enterprise Development, 2014. https://prosperitynow.org/files/resources/Upside_Down_to_Right-Side_Up_2014.pdf.

4 Will Fisher and Barbara Sard, "Chart Book: Federal Housing Spending is Poorly Matched to Need," Center on Budget and Policy Priorities, March 8, 2017. http://www.cbpp.org/research/housing/chart-book-federal-housing-spending-is-poorly-matched-to-need.

5 Congressional Budget Office, "Trends in Family Wealth, 1989 to 2013," August 2016. https://www.cbo.gov/sites/default/files/114th-congress-2015-2016/reports/51846-familywealth.pdf.

6 John Topoleski, "U.S. Household Savings for Retirement in 2010," Congressional Research Office, July 23, 2013. https://fas.org/sgp/crs/misc/R43057.pdf.

7 Nari Rhee, "Race and Retirement Insecurity in the United States," National Institute for Retirement Security, December 2013, 3. http://www.giaging.org/documents/NIRS_Report_12-10-13.pdf.

8 "Investing in Tomorrow: Helping Families Build Savings and Assets," Annie E. Casey Foundation, January 2016. www.aecf.org/resources/investing-in-tomorrow-helping-families-build-savings-and-assets/.

9 "A Look at the Shocking Student Debt Statistics for 2017," Student Loan Hero. https://studentloanhero.com/student-loan-debt-statistics/.

10 Josh Mitchell, "More than 40% of Student Borrowers Aren't Making Payments," *Wall Street Journal*, April 7, 2016. http://www.wsj.com/articles/more-than-40-of-student-borrowers-arent-making-payments-1459971348.

11 Jesse Rothstein and Cecilia Elena Rouse,

"Constrained After College: Student Loans and Early Career Occupational Choices," National Bureau of Economic Research. NBER Working Paper No. 13117. May 2007.

12 Dora Gicheva, "Does the Student-Loan Burden Weigh into the Decision to Start a Family?" University of North Carolina at Greensboro, March 2011. Also see Jennifer M. Shand, "The Impact of Early-Life Debt on the Homeownership Rates of Young Households: An Empirical Investigation," Federal Deposit Insurance Corporation, November 2007. Federal Deposit Insurance Corporation (FDIC).

13 Michael Mitchell, Michael Leachman, and Kathleen Masterson, "Funding Down, Tuition Up: State Cuts to Higher Education Threaten Quality and Affordability at Public Colleges," Center on Budget and Policy Priorities, August 15, 2016. http://www. cbpp.org/sites/default/files/atoms/files/5-19-16sfp. pdf.

14 Elizabeth McNichol, "Many States Tax Inherited Wealth," Center on Budget and Policy Priorities, December 9, 2015. http://www.cbpp.org/research/ many-states-tax-inherited-wealth.

15 Elizabeth McNichol, "State Estate Taxes: A Key Tool for Broad Prosperity," Center on Budget and Policy Priorities, May 11, 2016. http://www.cbpp. org/research/state-budget-and-tax/state-estate-taxes-a-key-tool-for-broad-prosperity.

16 John R. Burbank and Marilyn Watkins, "Washington's Estate Tax: Revenue for Higher Education and Early Learning," Economic Opportunity Institute,

February 24, 2010. www.research.policyarchive.org/95802.pdf.

17 See Bill Gates, Sr., "A GI Bill for the Next Generation," *Houston Chronicle,* June 22, 2004. http://www.chron.com/opinion/outlook/article/It-s-time-for-a-GI-Bill-for-the-next-generation-1504916.php.

18 "College for All Bill," introduced in 2017. https://www.sanders.senate.gov/download/college-for-all-act?inline=file.

19 See the Inclusive Prosperity Act of 2017. https://www.sanders.senate.gov/download/inclusive-prosperity-act-fact-sheet?inline=file.

20 Zachary Crockett, "San Francisco Just Offered Free College Tuition to All Its Residents," *Vox*, February 8, 2017. http://www.vox.com/policy-and-politics/2017/2/8/14545614/san-francisco-free-college-tuition.

21 Chuck Collins, Conor Kenny, Lee Farris, and Lincoln Taylor, "Spending Millions to Save Billions: The Campaign of the Super Wealthy to Kill the Estate Tax," Public Citizen & United for a Fair Economy, April 2006. http://www.citizen.org/documents/EstateTaxFinal.pdf.

22 2017 Infrastructure Report Card, American Society of Civil Engineers. http://www.infrastructurereportcard.org. Also see their report, "Failure to Act: Closing the Infrastructure Investment Gap for America's Economic Future," American Society of Civil Engineers, 2016. http://www.infrastructurereportcard.org/wp-content/uploads/2016/10/ASCE-Failure-to-Act-2016-FINAL.pdf.

23 See CarbonTracker, at: http://www.carbontracker.org/report/carbon-bubble/.

24 International Monetary Fund, "Is It Time for an Infrastructure Push? The Macroeconomic Effects of Public Investment," *World Economic Outlook*, October 2014, pp. 75–114. http://www.imf.org/external/pubs/ft/weo/2014/02/pdf/c3.pdf.

25 Robert Pollin and Brian Callaci, "A Just Transition for U.S. Fossil Fuel Industry Workers," *American Prospect*, July 6, 2016. http://prospect.org/article/just-transition-us-fossil-fuel-industry-workers.

26 WealthX, "Private Jets and the Ultra Wealthy," April 2016. http://www.wealthx.com/private-jets-ultra-wealthy/.

27 See Chuck Collins, "Can We Earn a Living on a Living Planet?" *American Prospect*, October 13, 2014. http://prospect.org/article/must-environmentalists-and-labor-activists-find-themselves-odds-each-other.

28 About the Alaska Permanent Fund. http://dividendsforall.net/the-alaska-model/.

29 Christine Emba, "Universal Basic Income," *Washington Post*, September 28, 2015. https://www.washingtonpost.com/news/in-theory/wp/2015/09/28/universal-basic-income-a-primer/?utm_term=.b8a69b71f807.

30 Ashifa Kassam, "Ontario Plans to Launch Universal Basic Income Trial Run This Summer," *Guardian*, April 24, 2017. https://www.theguardian.com/world/2017/apr/24/canada-basic-income-trial-ontario-summer?CMP=Share_iOSApp_Other.

31 Andy Stern with Lee Kravitz, *Raising the Floor: How a Universal Basic Income Can Renew Our Economy and Rebuild the American Dream*. Public Affairs, 2016.

Conclusion: Toward Equality

1 Sam Pizzigati, *Greed and Good: Understanding and Overcoming the Inequality That Limits Our Lives*. Apex Press, 2004, p. viii.